TAILS OF THE CITY

TAILS OF THE CITY

Confessions of a Manhattan Pet Vet
TOM DeVINCENTIS

Preface by Carolyne Roehm

Illustrations by BILL CHARMATZ

Glitterati
INCORPORATED

New York, New York

First published in the United States of America in 2008 by

New York, New York

Glitterati Incorporated
225 Central Park West
New York, New York 10024
www.GlitteratiIncorporated.com

First edition, 2008

Design by Sarah Morgan Karp, smk-design.com

Library of Congress Cataloging-in-Publication data is available from the Publisher.

Hardcover ISBN 13: 978-0-9793384-3-4

Printed and bound in China by Hong Kong Graphics & Printing Ltd.

10 9 8 7 6 5 4 3 2 1

Dedicated to my family, both human and animal, and to Tina, who taught me so much about love.

At the end of the day, no matter what happens at least I have my dog.

—Ancient Greek philosopher

Contents

Tails of the City

P r e f a c e

He is your friend, your partner, your defender, your dog. You are his life, his love, his leader. He will be yours, faithful and true, to the last beat of his heart. You owe it to him to be worthy of such devotion. —Unknown

After reading this collection of beautiful stories, one knows that veterinarian Tom DeVincentis is "worthy of such devotion." In New York City, a place obsessed with money, power, and getting ahead, how wonderful and reassuring it is to share the tales of this caring vet and his courageous patients. For those of us who love animals and understand what an integral part they play in our lives, this book teaches us how to cope with their loss.

I have had many dogs—nine at this moment—and Tom's lesson of loving and letting go is invaluable. My dogs are my family, my loves. They make me laugh and, oh, how they have made me cry and grieve when they go. I have often thought about how I am more empathetic to animals than to humans, and I'm certainly more forgiving when a puppy chews a Manolo Blahnik shoe or an antique chair leg. If a human committed an analogous infraction, they would be booted out the door!

My only regret with my animals, and that includes my cats and horses as well as my pups, is that they cannot speak. I talk to mine all of the time and how I wish they could respond, especially when they're sick and in pain. I wish I could explain that a car is a dangerous thing and that dashing into the road after a squirrel is forbidden. I have lost pets to old age and to disease but the worst experience is to lose them to tragedy. Last year, my beloved Wheaton Terrier was killed by a truck—I wished it had hit me as well. How I wish I'd had Tom's book to read at that time; it would have been a solace to my grief. Sharing stories of his and his patients' dogs, he teaches us the inevitability of our short but sweet time together with the animals we love. His empathy, kindness, and skill as a veterinarian radiate throughout this wonderful collection.

I was almost afraid to read this book because someone who knows my tenderness for animals said it would make me cry. It did . . . but it also made me laugh, and with Tom's wise words I appreciated all the more the amazing bond between we humans and all those four-legged creatures that add so much to our lives.

— Carolyne Roehm

Introduction: Taking Pause

After practicing veterinary medicine for over twenty-five years, it sometimes amazes me that the sight of an awkward, fuzzy puppy walking the streets of New York City can still make me smile. When I started writing this book, I was at a crossroads in my career. Although I still learned something new every day, much of my work was repetitious. After all, ear cleanings, vaccinations, and dentistry are hardly the stuff of dream fulfillment.

In New York City, company CEOs, investment bankers, and hedge fund managers are the financial captains of the universe. High-profile magazine editors, fashion designers, models, and interior designers represent the city's glam factor. In this social milieu, I questioned the importance of my contribution to the world, or at least society's appreciation of it. Even though my work was significant and sometimes made the difference between life and death, I was uneasy with my place in a city where the art of the deal was more often than not lauded over and celebrated.

I often wondered if living in a big city bred a particular clientele that was exceptionally demanding and neurotic—in short, a clientele that had become more and more difficult to deal with. Perhaps I was simply burned-out. Maybe I would have been happier in a different setting where life moved at a slower pace—somewhere like Ohio, my home state. Or perhaps I had chosen the wrong career entirely. I had countless questions with no definitive answers but I kept returning, again and again, to a burning one: Did I want to continue my work as a veterinarian?

On the surface, *Tails of the City* is a simple collection of stories about pets. While there are a few stories from my childhood, the majority presented here are set against the New York City backdrop, my home for the past two decades. Besides chronicling the lives of my patients, I've also looked at the intense personal relationships I've shared with my own pets. Each dog I've lived with and loved was my constant companion, my most consistent relationship, my steady anchor for that fifteen-year span that is the short, sweet life of dogs.

I have come to view the cycle of love and loss that any owner feels with his/her pet as an accelerated version of the human condition, one that encompasses everything from infancy to youth to maturity to old age and eventually death. Certain stages of a pet's life resonate more strongly with our own, depending on where we are within the scope of our own development and maturation. A toddler, for example, is infinitely fascinated with puppies or kittens while a young couple's first pet acts as a kind of "practice session," a surrogate child for the baby that may (or may not) be on the way. Within this animal-human relationship, we play the part of parent, knowledgeable of our mortality in a way that our pets, thankfully, remain blissfully unaware. Instead, they exist child-like and in the moment. We nurture, protect, discipline, and, in the end, say good-bye to our pets. Each of these stories touches on any one—or sometimes all—of these aspects of the animal-human bond.

In the process of writing *Tails of the City*, I have been reminded of the reason I became a vet in the first place. My place as a veterinarian is to bear witness to the enduring and unconditional love shared between human and animal. I consider it a rare privilege and honor to be part of this amazing cycle of life for so many animal and human friends for so many years. I am in the unique position to say that I love what I do, and this is a very rare gift indeed, no matter the city one lives in.

This collection is the story of my life.

—Tom DeVincentis

I   S A M : My Other Brother

I was in the fifth grade at Saint Henry's Catholic School in Cleveland, Ohio, and like most kids I had lobbied for a dog of my own for a long time. The fact that my older brother's dog, a collie named Bonnie, had become difficult to handle made my quest even harder. Sadly, Bonnie eventually broke off her leash and ran away. My resident population of white mice changed my luck. The day their glass aquarium slipped from its shelf and broke—with the subsequent recapture of only seventeen of the twenty-one mice—was the day I made a deal with my parents: If I gave my remaining mice to the local pet shop, could I get a dog? Mom gave in.

I made all the usual promises about feeding, walking, bathing, and otherwise taking full responsibility for the dog. I don't remember requesting any special breed—any dog would do. Perhaps Mom was ready for a puppy because my younger brother was already five years old, and the way things were going between Mom and Dad there weren't going to be any more human babies in our household. It seems strange to me now that I didn't help pick out the dog or go with Mom to bring him to our house, but I do remember waiting for them to come home. Mom drove a white 1958 Ford Fairlane convertible, and I can recall the precise moment on that fateful afternoon when she pulled into the driveway with the fruit of my campaigning. I ran outside and opened the passenger door. There on the front seat sat an eight-week-old chocolate-brown miniature poodle. We put him down on the lawn next to the house and the bright fall sunlight lit up his rich brown fur and innocent hazel-colored eyes. I loved him in an instant, and I loved Mom for getting him for me. He was quizzical and tentative. Taken from his Mom, waiting to forge a bond, he was probably a little nervous, too.

I never thought much about him being a poodle, and that to some of my friends he was more of a girl's dog than a boy's. We kept him shaggy, but occasionally Mom took him to the groomer for the Royal Dutch Clip. Mom named him Sam and had deliberately selected a male dog. Her selection wasn't surprising as we were a family of three boys. But I remember thinking that Mom should have picked a female pup so she wouldn't have been the only girl in the family. I think she often felt lonely.

It didn't take long for Sam to become part of the family. At first, he lived in the kitchen with a gate to keep him in, but he was soon sleeping upstairs in the bedroom I shared with my brothers. He usually slept in bed with me, but sometimes he slept with my other brothers, too. Although he was supposed to be my responsibility, Mom almost always fed him, and she spent the day with him since we were at school. But whenever he got sick or had an accident, it was my job to take care of him. Cleaning up after Sam never bothered me. If he vomited after raiding a neighbor's garbage can, it wasn't nearly as bad as when one of my brothers had a stomach virus and threw up. That bothered me.

In the 1960s, not many dog owners neutered their dogs, and hardly anyone fenced their yards, so that meant a lot of dogs roamed the neighborhood looking for female dogs or scavenging for food; Sam was no exception. My little brother and I, either with or without the help of our friends, would often have to cut through neighbors' yards and gardens yelling, "Sam, Sam, Sam!" Occasionally, Mom would drive us in the convertible to look for him, even though she said it was our fault for letting him off the leash or for not closing the aluminum screen door. On one occasion, I remember that we couldn't find Sam and he was out for a whole night, but he eventually came home on his own. Even that didn't teach us to control his roaming. The way I saw it was that he occasionally needed his freedom—and, in fact, really wanted it—so it was difficult to deny his impulse to roam.

Like most siblings, my brother and I fought a lot. Sam would usually join in on the roughhousing. I would invariably end up with my face pushed down into the carpet or into the grass, my arms pinned behind my back, my younger brother jumping on me. The yelling and horseplay would send Sam into a frenzy, and he would pull my pants leg, often biting me in his excitement. I always felt betrayed when he did this—after all, I took care of him the most. Now, however, I think he was trying to save me by pulling me away from my brothers. He was trying to keep me out of harm's way.

Sam hated being alone, which thankfully didn't happen very often. On Sundays, though, our family usually went for a drive in the country and out to dinner. Such outings frequently ended in fights between my mother and father, or among us boys. When Sam was left alone, he would jump on the knotty pine cocktail table that was in front of our plastic-covered Early American sofa. From that vantage point, he had a full view of the driveway and the street. Mom had spent a lot of time and money decorating that room, and it irked her to see paw prints or, worse, scratches on the furniture. I remember quietly praying after these disastrous car rides that our headlights wouldn't catch the flash of Sam's retinas as he gazed out the picture window, looking for us from his perch.

From time to time, Sam would wet our expensive all-wool carpet while we were away. When that happened, Sam was accused of doing spite work, and I had to listen to Mom's threats about getting rid of "that dog." Sam and I would trudge off to bed together. He was happy—blissfully ignorant—but I was afraid of the consequences and upset that Mom was angry at both Sam and me. Sometimes I would lie in bed and dramatically fantasize about the day when Mom or Sam would no longer be around. I used to pray that I'd die first because I didn't think I could stand the pain of losing either one of them.

Once, my friends and I took Sam swimming. There was a creek about a mile away from our house that had a few places where the water was deep enough to go swimming. Everyone knows that dogs can automatically swim, but we decided to prove it with Sam. I can't believe it now, but I actually threw my own dog into the water. His head went down last, but he sank under the surface without much of a struggle. After waiting for what seemed like forever, I was about to go in after him when he came up doing a lopsided kind of doggie paddle.

I could see the panic in his face. His body looked strained as he twisted and thrashed about in the water. Then he finally found his footing on the shallow bank, climbed out, and shook himself off. I felt like a traitor—a real Benedict Arnold. It amazed me that I could have been so mean to someone I loved so much. Needless to say, I never made him swim again. Dogs being more forgiving than humans, Sam didn't hold it against me. Or at least I don't think he did.

During my life with Sam, I decided I wanted to be a veterinarian. I used to go along on his infrequent visits to the vet's office, and I was impressed by the veterinarian who took care of him. Around this time in my life, I escalated my animal campaigning to the level of horse ownership, which would come later. Don't worry, I wasn't going to trade Sam in for a horse.

As the years rolled by, Sam started having more accidents, both upstairs on the bedroom's wooden floor and also on the wall-to-wall Armstrong carpeting, which was, by that time, a mess. Sam would jump into our bathtub in the middle of the night and scratch at the drain. I thought it was funny and smart that he knew how to get me to turn on the faucet to give him a drink of water. Even though I wanted to be a vet, I didn't realize he was drinking too much water. No one else

in our family did, either. When we took Sam in for an exam, we were told he had the beginning stages of kidney disease, and that he probably had it because we hadn't ever cleaned his teeth, which were pretty smelly. We could no longer blame poor Sam for his accidents, but that didn't make Mom feel any better about the carpet or the smell. She pretty much wanted Sam to go, which put a lot of pressure on me.

As it turned out, she was the one who left. She divorced Dad, which was a brave thing to do in 1962 in the Midwest. I think I was the only kid in my school whose parents had split up—at least it felt like that at the time. I didn't want her to go, but I actually understood how lonely she was. She spent night after night sitting in the dark, screened-in porch smoking cigarettes and drinking by herself, waiting for Dad to come home. The glow of her cigarette would light up her face, and

Sam would keep her company, patiently sitting beside her on the chaise lounge. During those times, I think Mom loved Sam despite the mess he'd made of her living room.

When Mom left, everything changed. My brothers and I were forced to grow up quickly. We stayed with Dad, who remarried on the last day of the year so he could claim his new wife as a tax deduction. Mom remarried, too, and surprised me by getting a female Boston terrier with her new husband. Sam's position was once again secure, since no new stepmom in her right mind would threaten to take her stepson's dog away.

By 1963, my campaigning for a horse paid off. While I still loved Sam, my attention shifted to a two-year-old racing thoroughbred named Ornery Mike. By that time, too, my sights were firmly set on vet school, and I spent all my spare time at the racetrack. I can't remember much of my life with Sam during this time period. I know that I loved him, and that when I put my arms around him he felt a lot bonier than he used to.

The years rolled by quickly, and soon my friends and I couldn't think about anything except graduation and our bright futures. We didn't understand just what we were about to leave behind; we didn't realize the foolishness of wanting to rush through our childhoods. I couldn't anticipate nor fathom how difficult if was going to be to leave Sam for college; dogs weren't allowed in the dorms at Ohio State. My younger brother was still in junior high so Sam would have some company, but Dad and Ruth, my stepmom, didn't make much of a fuss over Sam.

I was accepted into Ohio State University College of Veterinary Medicine in an accelerated undergraduate program after less than two years in college. Organic chemistry separates the men from the boys, however, and I failed the first midterm to my great surprise. If I failed the second midterm I would only have the final to redeem myself, and my acceptance into vet school might have to be postponed. The night that I was cramming for the exam, I received the phone call.

I don't remember if it was Dad or Ruth who gave me the news but I do recall that I wasn't able to study anymore that night. Sam had fallen asleep behind the Barker Lounger in the living room and had not woken up. Stunned by intense emotional pain, I made it to the test the next day but walked out early, somehow managing to earn a passing grade. I don't know what Dad did with Sam's body, and now that I think of it, there is no one left in my family to ask.

Years later, I had a conversation with Mom about dogs. She had retired to Florida and after having a succession of various breeds, she had settled on owning Shih Tzus. She confessed that Bonnie, my older brother's dog, hadn't really run off, but instead had been given away. I kept that secret from my brother, but now I sometimes wonder if there was any foul play involved in Sam's demise. After all, he was only ten years old when he'd fallen asleep and never woke up.

Like my Mom, I have had a few lifetimes with dogs since Sam. His memory is blurred by the others who came after him, but Sam will always hold a special place in my heart because he was my first dog.

II ORNERY MIKE: At the Gate

A bright shaft of light from the hayloft window illuminated the gray colt's head, which seemed large for his body. Dimly backlit by the glow from a cracked stall window covered with cobwebs, he was short and thick through his chest. A dark gray forelock fell on the white, wide blaze, accentuating his Roman nose. His white-rimmed eyes scanned the uneven dirt floor as he reached down to nuzzle the fetid straw at his feet, his nose steaming with each breath. We were definitely more interested in him than he was in us.

"His older brother broke his maiden on his second start last year and finished in the money on his last two outings," Whitey Whitesides told us. He explained the colt's parentage with no shortage of enthusiasm. "His sire was a son of Solar, one of the best distance studs on the East Coast in the late 1940s. His dam comes from a long line of stake horses going back to Bold Venture. I think this colt can do anything." He had me convinced. My father, a plumbing contractor who had met Whitey at the Dew Drop Inn, a popular haunt located just outside the entrance gate of the Thistle Downs Racetrack, was listening intently.

Whitey's monologue continued as I held my breath in anticipation. At thirteen, I was on course to becoming a veterinarian. My experiences with animals had already included mice, Sam, parakeets, a baby alligator my parents had purchased for me on a trip to Florida, turtles, tadpoles, salamanders, and frogs. My world had been transformed at age eleven, however, after reading Walter Farley's *The Black Stallion* and all of its sequels. Other books followed during my enthusiastic study of breeds, anatomy, tack, gait patterns, and horse husbandry. The previous summer I had ridden for two weeks at the Catholic Youth Organization Camp, and occasionally I'd been able to convince Dad to take me on a one-hour trail ride at the local stable. For two years, I had regularly and relentlessly begged Dad for a horse, just as I had begged Mom for my first dog, Sam.

At a dilapidated farm in rural Ohio, I crossed my fingers as the deal was brokered. The smell of ammonia hung in the frigid barn air. I had no idea how much $600 was worth, but it seemed a small price to pay for a chance at fame and fortune in thoroughbred racing. Of course, it was Dad's money, but it represented the sum of all my hopes and dreams. I couldn't have been happier as I looked at my new horse.

The colt's name had been recorded in the thoroughbred registry at birth, and though I would have chosen something more noble sounding than Ornery Mike, it couldn't be changed. In the spring, Ornery Mike would start training as a two-year-old at Whitey's small but elegantly named Swan Creek Stables, which consisted mostly of older claimers. Claimers are horses for sale before each race at a specific price, and while they're not elite, some can carry high prices.

All racehorses, no matter when they are born, are automatically considered one year older on New Year's Day. Ornery Mike, who would not actually be two until the following fall, would be at a disadvantage when competing with more physically developed two-year-olds who had been born a full six months or more before him. The fact that Ornery Mike was young and small hit a chord with me, as I was the youngest person in my class and consequently one of the smallest. The possibility that he might run as a claimer filled me with a sense of unease.

Every Saturday and Sunday at 6:00 AM, Whitey pulled into our driveway and took me to the barn. Along the way, we'd stop to pick up crullers and coffee for him and milk for me at the nearby Seven Gables restaurant where his wife, Gladys, worked as a waitress. Whitey always wore the same outfit: pressed khakis and a blue cardigan sweater over long underwear and a work shirt. His fedora covered half of his brow and never left his head. Paddock boots and suspenders completed the look.

Whitey never called me by my name. Instead, he always referred to me as the Kid. He took great pride in my developing equine and card playing skills. Gladys and Whitey didn't have children, and I became a surrogate grandchild of sorts. Since I had no previous experience with horses, Whitey taught me everything I needed to know, like how to approach a horse from the side and not from the front as horses can't see well straight ahead; how to crosstie a horse by his halter; and how to feed a horse from the feed bucket and not from your hand, else you might lose your fingers. The list went on and on. I figured out pretty quickly that horses are not large dogs as much as I wanted to treat Ornery Mike as a house pet.

Since spring training didn't start until March, Ornery Mike spent the winter on a lunge rope, reducing his baby fat. Individually or in twos, the horses were turned out in the paddocks that fronted the barn. Ornery Mike was usually turned out separately because he was a stallion and could fight with the others, many of whom were old stablemates, and had raced as claimers under Whitey for many years.

After mucking the stalls, we fed the horses, brushed them, and cleaned their hooves. Then we turned our attention to sweeping the dirt floor of the barn. In my youthful fervor, I concentrated on removing every spare shaft of straw caught in the cracked, uneven corridor floor. Then we worked on the leather tack, which was barely used in the winter but saddle-soaped nonetheless to keep it pliable and ready for spring, when we would move the horses down the road to Thistle Downs.

After the weekend chores, several locals would drop by for hours of horse talk and pinochle or gin rummy. Being young and shy, I was silent, and concentrated on the cards while I listened to the horse tales. Cigarette and pipe smoke filled the cold winter air while we played. Jockeys in the winner's circle smiled down at us from the photos on the walls, their faces flushed and beaming with pride, fueling my fantasies about Ornery Mike and his potential. I also tried hard to learn how to play cards well because I felt it was a necessary skill to acquire on my way toward becoming a successful trainer.

Whitey often thumbed through his cards and invariably complained that he didn't have "a pair or a possible." He cursed to high heaven when his discards were picked up by another player. He would string together a litany of profanities when someone tabled his cards and declared gin. "That's all she wrote," he'd mutter, pushing his chair away from the table. "It's colder than a witch's tit in here," he'd say, whatever that meant, or he'd yell about the poor reception on the radio. He was always talking, complaining, criticizing, and cursing. The other players would answer and agree or disagree with swear words of their own. My Catholic school boy ears eventually dulled to this profane onslaught and no longer burned red to hear misogynistic innuendoes and other outbursts hurled back and forth between the weathered cronies. Whitey's invectives were the most blistering whenever I won, his face reddening, his thin lips spewing out some choice words. But as soon as we began the next hand, he bragged to the other guys about how well the Kid could play.

In April, it was time to start training. Ornery Mike had grown accustomed to being lunged with a bit in his mouth and a saddle on his back, but he'd only occasionally had a rider. By now I was head over heels in horse heaven and felt bonded to Ornery Mike who I was sure had some affection for me, too. After all, he kicked and bit me less often than he did the others who tried to handle him. He was living up to the "ornery" part of his name, turning to nip anyone who tightened his girth and occasionally rearing to strike with a foreleg—the most dangerous of equine bad manners.

Whitey met this behavior with angry discipline and corporal punishment, yanking the lead chain on Ornery

Mike's muzzle or flogging him with a long leather shank. Definitely an old-school trainer and not a horse whisperer, Whitey believed the relationship between man and horse was but a contest of wills. Fear was a training weapon to be wielded with abandon; you couldn't let a horse get away with anything.

Ornery Mike slowly adjusted, bucking and head-tossing a little less each time he was mounted. Gradually the terror in his white-rimmed eyes gave way to resignation. He settled down for his early morning workouts around the track, learned not to break from the starting gait before it was time, and eventually didn't mind being bathed and walked around the shed row to cool off.

Mornings on the track at Thistle Downs were magical. Before the sun came up, Whitey and I had breakfast at the track cafeteria. By then, I had decided that I wanted to become a jockey, and I weighed myself each morning while pleading with God to keep me from growing too much. Contemplating deep-fried crullers and crispy, fat-laden hash browns versus a grapefruit and hard-boiled eggs, I struggled to make the less fattening choice. Whitey would order eggs over easy and the runny, glistening, half-curdled whites would send shivers up my spine, stoking my gag reflex. It's a wonder I didn't end up with an eating disorder.

Sitting together, the Old Man and the Kid, we would survey the room, Whitey filling me in on the history and other details of each character. Jockeys, grooms, exercise boys, bookies, farriers, and track officials filled the noisy, fluorescent-lit cafeteria in that convivial predawn hour. After breakfast, we went to our shed. Underneath a sloping roof was a well-worn path where the horses were walked to cool down after races and workouts. Parallel rows of sheds in groups occupied various corners of the track property, housing several hundred thoroughbreds and their hay, straw, and tack. Mountains of manure were piled here and there. Owners, trainers, agents, handicappers, farriers, tooth floaters (people who file sharp edges off horses' teeth), and an occasional back-rail loafer or sports reporter commingled in a world in which I was more an observer than a participant.

The racetrack was most alive between 6:00 AM and 9:00 AM, when most of the exercising, lunging, ponying around the track, blowouts, and "breezing" took place. Ornery Mike and the other horses were led around the track at a canter or slow gallop by an exercise pony horse and rider. Pony horses are full-sized horses and are usually larger and calmer than the thoroughbreds they help control and support. On other mornings, the horses would be lunged on a rope in a circle off the track. This was something I was allowed to do. For twenty or thirty minutes, I would lead a horse in a tight circle around me, and the sun would play off his musculature. The whole experience was hypnotizing. During those sessions, I felt utterly and thoroughly a part of the racing world, and that was a heady feeling.

The most exciting track workouts were those with the exercise boys. For these workouts, horses were galloped at a steady pace or "blown out" and urged to run an all-out sprint of several furlongs in preparation for an upcoming race. I stood at the rail with Whitey, his stopwatch in hand, listening to him comment on each performance. When my horse ran through the paces, I hung on Whitey's every word as he described Ornery Mike's "way of going," or his being a "daisy cutter," or being "corded up," his veins bulging from exertion. The rising sun, the cool early breezes, the rush of the hurtling horses—all of these images forged indelible memories of my gray colt at work in the steel-purple dawn.

Eventually, the morning activity would end. Back at the barn, the horses were bathed and then walked under the shed roof until they were sufficiently cooled down. As we walked, I sang the choruses to whatever tune I heard as we passed the radio playing in the tack room. Cooling out horses was a monotonous job. After the horses had been fed and watered, their day was completed by 10:00 AM, unless they were called on to race later. Our small stable usually entered no more than one to two races a week.

Race days found me with brush in hand, grooming Ornery Mike until he shone. Even though he wasn't scheduled to head out to the track, I'd push a curry comb in tireless circles until his hair shed off in silver tufts and a fine powder rose from his skin, covering my fingers in a slick film. I'd weave and unweave his mane into a braid or a topknot, or practice tying his long tail under a bandage wrap. I was preparing for the day we'd be racing and wouldn't want mud or water from the track to add extra weight to his tail. Alone in the stall with Mike, his head in a hay bag, I'd feel my cautious fear of him giving way to trust. Sometimes, as he lay sleeping in his box stall, I'd sit down and lean my back and shoulders against his withers, his warm heavy weight radiating through me, filling me with comfort.

Some days, getting up at 5:00 AM took its toll, and by the afternoon I'd be napping high up on the stacked bales of hay and straw, which were piled nearly ceiling high in the feed room. From this perch I could look down on the rows of stalls and listen to the buglers call to the track. Every twenty-five minutes, the roar of the crowd in the grandstands welcomed a new winner crossing the wire. I impatiently waited for the day when it would be our turn.

On other afternoons, the leather-aproned farrier would visit to outfit the horses in new shoes or the veterinarian would come, his station wagon filled with aromatic medications for wormings or vaccinations. I would look on in amazement as the farrier trimmed and sliced hooves and then nailed aluminum shoes into the feet of a patiently standing thoroughbred. I watched tattooers apply black-inked needles to the inside upper lips of horses for identification. At first, all of this was new and remarkable and, to my child's eyes, somewhat barbaric and cruel. Soon, however, I didn't consider it unusual when an eight-foot-long rubber tube was passed through a horse's nostril and into his stomach to administer a worming, while the horse was made to stand still by wrapping a twitch—a metal chain—around his sensitive upper lip. I no longer blinked when the vet's rubber-gloved arm disappeared under the tail of a calmly standing mare so that he could palpitate her ovaries.

I observed a world that excited and fascinated me even as I felt distanced and repelled by its practicalities. I slowly became aware that the racetrack had a hard edge that went beyond the practicalities of equine husbandry. Winning

meant everything. Underneath the excitement, lurked an unexpressed, quiet sense of desperation. I didn't spend too much time thinking about that, enthralled as I was by the romance of racing and eager to keep dreaming of a glorious future of fame and fortune.

Ornery Mike was shaping up and showing signs of promise in his early morning breezes. His older brother, who had won a race on only his second start, was consistently finishing in the money. It was time to enter Ornery Mike in his first race: six furlongs (three quarters of a mile) for two-year-old maidens at a claiming price of $2,500. Maidens were horses, both male and female, who had not yet won a race. I wasn't worried that Ornery Mike would be bought from under us since he was an unknown commodity, but in the back of my mind I knew that until he broke out of the arena of claimers, the lowest rung on the racing ladder, I would run the risk of suddenly losing him.

On race day, I woke ahead of the sound of the alarm clock and was waiting in the driveway well before Whitey pulled up to get me. I wondered if it was sacrilegious that I was reciting Hail Marys in the hopes of influencing the outcome of the race. Dad shared some of my anxiety because he was already feeling the financial pinch of training and maintaining a thoroughbred racehorse. Ownership was beginning to demand more money than he had anticipated (Whitey had probably lowballed the estimates), and he was looking for a little payback. Whitey, hoping to justify his choice of Ornery Mike, was also feeling pressure as he had not had many winners over the past several years. He knew his next step might be forced retirement or a move to Wheeling, West Virginia, where the least expensive of all the claimers ended up. Ornery Mike was the only one who wasn't worrying.

At mid-morning, after the other horses were bedded down for the day, I slipped into Ornery Mike's stall for a pre-race visit. He let me stroke his muzzle as I tried to convey my love for him, a knot of anticipation and dread in my stomach. I feared for his safety and his success. He would have my hope and devotion regardless of the outcome.

Several times that summer, while listening to the noise of the races as I dozed in the feed room, I'd heard the roaring crowd stop mid-race in a collective gasp as a horse and rider stumbled and fell to the turf. Over the gentle murmur of the fans the vet ambulance would approach the downed pair. When it ended well, the crowds would cheer wildly as horse and rider unfolded themselves and stood up, shaken but uninjured. As I reflected on this possibility, the romance of the race gave way to the fact that anything might happen: winning, losing, or injury. Ornery Mike, although he had trained at the starting gait and had breezed with companion horses around the track, did not know what he was facing. For all his toughness and orneriness, he was an innocent soul. True, horses seemed to enjoy running with other horses, but was it just a human conceit to say they enjoyed winning, or even knew they had won? I decided that although it might not be okay to pray for Ornery Mike to win, it would be all right to pray that he would be safe. I rubbed my palms against his eyes as he closed them and pushed into me, and I hoped for the best.

* * *

Our racing silks were large pink polka dots on a pale gray background—the only input Mom had offered aside from her fear for my safety. The colors complimented the horse's dappled gray coat, and I imagined the picture we would make in the winner's circle, smiles all around and Ornery Mike slick with sweat, nostrils flaring. During the walk from the barn, Ornery Mike knew something was up. Prancing and tossing his head, he arrived at the saddling paddock with a foamy white lather between his rear legs. As the saddle was lowered, he tried to swing away from it, and he turned to bite

Whitey as the girth was tightened. Though he wore blinders to prevent him from seeing horses come up from behind him, the whites of his eyes were glowing.

On the call to the post, he crab-stepped and salivated, and even attempted a few half-hearted bucks on his way to the gate. I silently hoped that all of this spent energy was just a fraction of what was stored inside. As the horses entered the gate, I found myself praying quietly.

As they broke, Ornery Mike came away with all the others, but his head tilted as he pulled and drifted, wasting time and ground. By the third furlong, he was second to last, the jockey flailing his whip and creating welts on Ornery Mike's rump. He continued to fall back and ended up finishing twenty lengths behind the winner, his dilated nostrils crimson red. It was all over in a minute. Whitey and Dad looked sad and stunned. There were excuses all around—bad rider, first start, wrong bit, wrong blinders. Wait until next time.

Ornery Mike was extremely agitated as I led him back to our shed. He anxiously pulled me in the direction of his stall, his home. He wanted to return to his herd, our ragtag band of aging, mostly futureless, often luckless horses living under the Swan Creek banner. Whispering to him all the way, stroking his neck, taking him in, I was relieved that the ordeal was finished, at least for today. After he was bathed, walked, and fed a warm bran mash, the next reality settled in. Ornery Mike and I were on borrowed time. More Hail Marys were in order. The irony that I had fed Sam canned kennel rations made in part with horsemeat did not escape me.

We needed a new game plan. Ornery Mike's bloodlines were those of distance horses whose best performances had been in races longer than a mile. Furthermore, many of his ancestors had been most successful on grass or on wet-to-muddy tracks. Ornery Mike would be trained for stamina—to go the distance. Grass was out of the question (there were only a few grass races and grass tracks) and the weather was unpredictable, but we could train him to be a contender in longer races that many of his two-year-old rivals would shun in their first campaign. With renewed hope, we continued our routine.

That June, Whitey had a win (first place) and a place (second place) with Barge In, the $1,200 claimer he'd picked up the previous fall. A rangy nine-year-old chestnut gelding, his bowed tendon cured by a pin-firing that winter, Barge In was a testimony to Whiteside's abilities to pick 'em. If this horse could do it, why couldn't Ornery Mike?

As the summer went on, Ornery Mike's workouts became longer and faster, and perhaps because he was more tired, his barn etiquette slightly improved. Less apt to kick or strike, he was still inclined to bite as his saddle girth was tightened or to nip the pony boy's leg as he was cantered around the track. The longer races weren't held until the end of the meet, so it was decided that he would be entered in one more six-furlong race to keep up his racing form and education.

The night before the race, there were thunderstorms, ensuring a soft-to-muddy track. As a result, expectations ran high on race day. Only eight horses were entered, so loading and breaking from the gait would be, we hoped, fast and simple. Ornery Mike was re-shod with cleated shoes to give him more traction in the mud. He would wear full rather than half blinders to force him to focus on only what was in front of him. I added a few Our Fathers to my usual Hail Marys.

Ornery Mike broke from the gait early and ran slightly off the pace of the frontrunner and four lengths behind. The field held the same position for the first four furlongs, and as they moved into the turn toward home, Whitey and Dad joined the heated crowd yelling with excitement. The pink-and-gray silks were easy to spot on the outside position as they came into the home stretch. My Hail Marys were flying hard and fast as we waited for the jockey to make his move. Come on, Ornery Mike!

But my prayers were not to be answered. As the frontrunner faltered and faded, the approaching pack closed around Ornery Mike, then passed him in a rush one furlong before the finish. We ended up seventh, just ahead of the horse that had led the pace. As the rider dismounted he told us that when he had asked Ornery Mike for more there "just wasn't any." When we pulled the blinders from his mud-splattered face, we noticed a trickle of crimson in his dilated nostrils. Ornery Mike was a bleeder. Capillaries had burst in his lungs, which had been overtaxed by his heart's effort. Crying, I led him back to the barn, the red stream now turning a pinkish meringue. Mucus and blood blended with the violent rush of air that flowed in and out of his nasal passages as he struggled to regain his wind. Tears and blood, mud and sweat—everything mixed together to accentuate my grief. I knew that time was closing in and that there was little room for further failure.

These days bleeders are treated with Lasix, a diuretic given before the race that causes fluids locked up in a horse's body tissues to be released and expelled in the urine. This lowers the horse's blood pressure and largely prevents bleeding. Almost all of the horses who ran in the Triple Crown races of the past few years have been on it at one point or another in their lives, although studies of its effectiveness vary. But in the 1960s, there were no real treatments except for various folk remedies. Ornery Mike's treatment was to inhale burning menthol or eucalyptus leaves ignited in a galvanized metal bucket, a blanket over his head to prevent the escape of the supposedly therapeutic smoke. His hoof beat would ring out as he fitfully kicked at the barn wall in protest over this cauterization of his lungs. It seemed as if we were burning incense in an offering to some equine god, but I had to put my faith in something. Ornery Mike's shoes were changed in order to take pressure off of a quarter crack that had developed in one of his hooves. And his snaffle bit would be adjusted, too.

And so, our hopes restored, Ornery Mike was entered into his longest race so far, a mile for two-year-old maidens, at his lowest claiming price of $1,200. This would be his last chance to prove himself for the year. It was late September, and the Cleveland meet ended by mid-October. A lot was riding on this race. Aside from the expense of boarding and training Ornery Mike, my Mom and Dad were more at odds than ever over the suitability and safety of a racetrack environment for a thirteen-year-old boy. Failure meant we'd have to face up to the end of all of our dreams. Ornery Mike didn't know he was carrying more than the 118-pound-jockey.

Ornery Mike broke from the gate and was in fourth position by the quarter pole, and there he stayed. The frontrunner held his lead for the entire race as the second and third horses alternately challenged each other. Ornery Mike ran without great effort, almost in slow motion. The pace was far from blistering—a mile in one minute and thirty-nine seconds—and the response from the crowd was lackluster. But Ornery Mike crossed the wire safely, winded but not bleeding, earning $65 for his efforts.

Whitey and Dad were mollified, if not overjoyed, and I was ecstatic, my faith in Ornery Mike's career having been restored. But my euphoria was short-lived. A few days later, we found him standing on his left foreleg. He had popped a shin splint on his right leg, which meant the end of his campaign as a two-year-old. He needed to rest for the remainder of the year so that his shin splints could be blistered, and he'd return to racing the following spring as a maiden three-year-old.

That winter was a tough one for Ornery Mike. Blistering his shin splint was a painful procedure—a caustic chemical spread over the already painful shin splint causes the skin to swell, bubble, and sometimes slough off. The inflammation caused by the blistering was supposed to bring an increase in circulation and thus aid the healing process. Also that winter, Whitey told Dad that he wanted to have Ornery Mike "cut," equine slang for castration, as the colt had discovered his sexuality. Male horses that have low potential for producing are often neutered to prevent them from fighting and flirting and to enhance their focus. I put up great resistance to this, romanticizing his stallion status and wanting to spare him from further pain. I held back tears as his lip was rolled up in the twitch, then a nerve block injected to anaesthetize the area as the veterinarian gelded him. What was most important was that we did everything we could to give Ornery Mike his best chance of having some success.

I never got to lead Ornery Mike into the winner's circle. Through my tenaciousness, we persevered for another two racing seasons, but Ornery Mike never broke his maiden or finished in the money again. All that I have left of him sits in a box somewhere—a chignon-shaped collection of his gray tail hair, a few darkened and cracked Polaroids, and some old racing forms. I was told he was given to an Amish couple in Pennsylvania who were anxious to train him as a carriage horse. Months later my uncle took me to visit him, but we were told he had kicked down his stall and had been given away once again. We were never able to trace him after that.

I hope Ornery Mike lived a long and productive life with someone who saw him as more than just a beast of burden. The statistics quoted by the Thoroughbred Race Horse Retirement Foundation are too awful to consider. My farewell to Ornery Mike was my farewell to most things equine. The business of horse racing being too practical for a nurturing personality, I turned my veterinary interest to small animal medicine. But who knows? Maybe someday I'll open a barn door and find that kid on the black stallion, that kid I once wanted to be.

III M A R G O T : The Dog of My Dreams

Surrounded by a group of enthusiastic veterinary students, who were clumsily attempting to improve their venpuncture skills, Zee trembled violently, causing the stainless-steel table to vibrate. Under the glare of the exam light, the poor dog looked helpless. A student tried to draw blood from her forelimb with a needle, while another restrained her head, and yet a third steadied her extended leg. Someone had tied a black rubber tourniquet tightly above her elbow. The table and floor were littered with bloodied alcohol swabs. The dog was too intimidated to protest. When her head was free, she cowered and looked away, gulping with fear. Caught up in their zeal for knowledge and thrilled to be working on a real patient, they were unaware of her anxiety and did little to comfort her.

Zee had been in the ward for several weeks, an adoption sign hanging above her cage. Normally Ohio State University didn't deal in pet adoptions, but Zee was there at the request of a friend of the assistant dean. At six years of age she had outgrown her usefulness in a breeding kennel, but her owner had not been able to face dropping her off at the local shelter or putting her down. The soft spot in his heart was not soft enough to cause him to elevate her to house-dog status upon her retirement. At the vet school, she was placed as part of my medical student caseload. I was in charge of her care and hoped to find her a new home by the end of the spring term when the majority of students left for summer break.

That afternoon, having just finished an introduction to surgery class, during which I learned how to make my first incision into living, breathing, anesthetized feline flesh, I was on my way home, exhilarated and exhausted. I noticed students surrounding Zee who was quivering. Surprised by the sight, I broke their silence by reminding them that they weren't allowed to practice procedures on Zee.

I carried her to the ward, cleaned her multiple puncture wounds with peroxide, and offered her a cardboard plate of dry kibble, which she was too shy to eat in front of me. Her life in the breeding kennel had left her with few social skills. Although her given name was Zee (perhaps for the silent "z" in Vizsla), she didn't respond to it.

Vizslas were relatively unknown in 1968 and were not at all popular in Columbus, Ohio. Bred as Hungarian hunting hounds, they have short rust-colored coats and large eyes, and they resemble their more widely known German cousin, the gray-coated Weimaraner. At forty pounds, Zee was small for her breed. Pendulous nipples bespoke her life as the mother of innumerable puppies.

As veterinary students, we were interested in the sickest patients, the cases we could most learn from. At first Zee held no special allure for me because she was physically healthy. To look at her, though, you couldn't help but feel sad. A pat on the head was a threat to her, and talking to her sweetly produced an occasional tiny ticktock of her metronome-like tail. With time, she began to respond to me by wagging her tail with some enthusiasm. Eventually she allowed me to pat her head or scratch her chin without flinching. Still avoiding any real eye contact, she would lean toward me ever so slightly as I rubbed, her rear leg reaching up to scratch when I found a spot that provoked her irrepressible tickle reflex.

On walks outside the clinic, Zee was especially sensitive to any loud noise or to the reflection of sunlight beaming off an approaching car. Afraid of her own shadow, she would cower and tremble as she pulled me back toward the safety of the building. In the clinic, she trembled and sat at the back of her crate and blinked apprehensively at any sight or sound. I could only comfort her by covering her with a blanket, under which she would stay for hours, waiting for her fear to pass.

A slow but steady stream of potential adopters visited Zee, but those who were taken by her comeliness could not engage her, even with kindness. Zee resolutely hung her head, refusing all approaches, having too little self-esteem to respond to encouragement. The spring term was coming to a close, and I placed my faith on a potential adopter I was to interview two weeks before the beginning of summer vacation.

Zee's last hope arrived in a broken-down pickup truck loaded with electrical supplies. The potential adopter told me he was looking for a dog to keep him company and guard his truck while he made supply deliveries. Sporting a tattoo of a dragon on his bicep, he told me he liked Zee's look and thought he could overcome her shyness. Zee, for her part, pretended he wasn't there. I couldn't imagine this shy hound guarding a truck nor could I overcome my growing fondness for Zee. I called him the next day to say Zee's owner had come forward to claim her. With that phone call, Zee became mine.

I vowed to restore her confidence and draw her out of her pathological shyness. I had no idea how ingrained her fears might be, but was confident that love and time could conquer all. I decided to change her name to one we could both respond to, feeling this would do no harm as she barely responded to her given name. When changing a dog's name, I usually recommend that one should choose something with the same number of syllables and a similar sound as the dog's original name—Beanie to Billie, Rusty to Dusty, et cetera.—so that the dog easily understands the new name and the change isn't too dramatic. In Zee's case, however, I wanted a Hungarian name to reflect her pedigree. My associations with the Hungarian culture were paprika and the Gabor sisters. Paprika was easy to eliminate. Eva, Zsa Zsa, and Magda were out of the question with the first name being too feminine and the others too difficult to pronounce. I decided to call her Margot.

With no small measure of trepidation, I brought Margot home with me. She had never lived in a home environment, and we were relative strangers to each other. Neither of us knew what to expect. Was she housebroken? Where would she sleep? Should I change her diet? Margot was the first dog

I'd had on my own. Even though Sam had been my first dog, he had mainly been Mom's responsibility. Margot was the first dog of my adult life.

Unsurprisingly, Margot dealt with her new environment by hiding. When I went out to run an errand, I would find her tucked under the bed or hiding in the bathtub behind the shower curtain. When we were together at home, I blocked off her hiding places, forcing her to be out in the open with me. She was still too shy to eat in front of me, so I would sit on the floor and feed her by hand. After she became accustomed to that, I let her sit by my side as I ate and fed her from the table, aware that I was teaching her a bad habit. I continued to comfort her by covering her with a blanket when she was frightened. At night, Margot slept under the comforter, fitting into the crook of my body.

I knew I was creating a monster by allowing such familiarity. As I often asked my clients with new puppies: Did they want to allow a dog into their bed for the next fifteen years? I admitted to myself that one day I might share my nights with somebody who preferred a dogless bed, but the initial arrangement meant that Margot and I slept soundly through the night.

We continued to build on our tentative bond based on food and security. She happily jumped into the bed at night to get safely under the covers, and rushed out into the open to be next to me whenever I sat down to eat. But she was always waiting for someone to drop a house on her and nervously reacted to loud sounds. She was especially fearful of shadows.

She avoided eye contact and could not be consoled. No matter what I did, Margot could not relax. I still hadn't reached that place in her heart where her trust outweighed her fear. She was still the primordial dog circling an ancient campfire, afraid to cross over into the glowing light of domesticity.

On our walks, it wasn't uncommon for people to greet us, and kneel to look into Margot's face, scratch behind her ears, and gently whisper to her. With time, she became more at ease with the attention, demurely lowering her head and no longer trembling as she leaned into me, reassuring herself with the physical contact.

At the end of our street was a field of grass, and there Margot rediscovered her hound instincts under an open sky, rolling in the grass, pushing her face along the ground, and acting like a normal, healthy dog, for all intents and purposes. The field's periphery was wooded, and there she often picked up a scent through the fallen leaves. It was clear that she was at her best in an outdoor environment with no loud noises to threaten her sense of well being.

After I graduated from veterinary school I moved to the most urban environment in the country: New York City. I lived in an apartment on the fourth floor of a brownstone building on East Seventy-second Street, not far from the office of my first job or Central Park. Climbing seventy-seven stairs for each of our four daily walks combined with various other outings kept Margot and me in very good shape. Margot adapted to the stairs but was easily bewildered by the sounds and sights of the busy, noisy city streets.

At times she was almost paralyzed by fear, and I often carried her most of the way to the park. Once she was away from the cars, noise, and commotion, she would audibly sigh and shake herself out from head to tail. She would drop and roll around in the grass or leaves and follow her nose on a long leash. In Central Park, the weight of her worries slipped away and her natural canine instincts trumped her insecurities.

Eventually she adjusted to concrete and picked up earthy scents from cracks in the sidewalks. We switched to a harness instead of a collar, as that gave her more contact with me through the leash, and she walked a little more bravely. But she always walked faster on the homeward stretch, ignoring several doormen who tried to befriend her by offering a kind word or treat. With time, Margot found an uneasy comfort zone. She felt safest with me in bed under the covers, where she would lick her forepaws for a few minutes and move to the top of my feet, grooming me. I wondered if she was giving in to some maternal nature as she took care of me, our roles temporarily reversed.

That summer I took a share in a group house on Fire Island, a long and narrow sandbar that separates the southern coast of Long Island from the Atlantic Ocean. Though Cleveland, my hometown, was located on Lake Erie, our family rarely took advantage of the water, and to live each weekend on the edge of the ocean was thrilling. My friends were very friendly to Margot, and I looked forward to an environment where the groceries were casually carted home in a red-flyer wagon. Shoes were optional, and life was lived in a bathing suit.

We took weekly trips to Fire Island by bus and ferry boat, with Margot buried underneath my seat for an hour and a half. As we approached the narrow barrier reef of summer cottages and wooden boardwalks, Margot would sniff the sea air and begin her metamorphosis into the confident canine that she actually was deep down inside. Once on the island, she would run along the beach, roll in decaying vegetation or putrefying sea life, and dig deep holes in the sand in search of something only she knew might be there. As in the story *Flowers for Algernon*, at the end of each weekend spent at the edge of a limitless ocean horizon, she returned to her emotionally crippled state upon arrival in the city.

Margot never had a breakthrough or recovery, and remained tentative and afraid her entire life. Perhaps Manhattan was not the best place for her, but it was where I worked. At first she was my only friend in New York, though we soon made a widening circle of acquaintances while on our walks through the park. New York dog owners share an enthusiastic camaraderie, and I rarely went out for a walk without someone asking about Margot's breed, age, or temperament.

I made sure, as best as I could, that she had her special time each day to follow her nose along the East River Promenade, a charming strip of park that parallels the FDR Drive. There were occasional canine escapades she enjoyed more than others, times when her cropped tail timidly vibrated in a visceral response to a dog that she could appreciate more than others. We rarely encountered other Vizslas, but Margot's reaction to the occasional Weimaraner was always the strongest.

I coped with her fears by avoiding the noisier truck-filled avenues when possible and walked her at quieter times of the day. I learned to live with her limitations, to love her for what she was, and not to yearn for what she could have been. I loved her because she was mine to love, and if love could not conquer all, then love itself would have to be enough. Attending to her neediness fulfilled my desire to nurture. Some friends regarded her as an albatross, an anchor that kept me from leading a normal New York City life, as I was inclined not to leave her when she was cowering under a blanket or hiding in a closet, which was often.

By the time she was fifteen years old, many of Margot's fears had diminished. Life on the twenty-third floor of a Manhattan high-rise was hardly a peaceful oasis by anyone's standards. The concrete canyons of the city magnified the noise from horns, sirens, and garbage trucks at street level. Margot still preferred to snuggle under a blanket rather than to lie on the floor or even on my bed. Although most of her life she had tremendous control of her bladder, she could no longer hold it overnight, and soiled the carpet, elevator, and lobby. I started carrying her in the elevator we shared with my handsomely dressed neighbors. The neighbors voiced their concerns, asking, "Is she sick?" "Can't she walk?" "How old is that dog?" Some people were sympathetic while others disapproved of her condition and averted their eyes or shook their heads.

Arthritic changes in her hips made walks around the block impossibly long. Laying down newspapers over a plastic liner proved insufficient, and the wood floor warped and became discolored. I burned patchouli-scented candles to cover the odor. Margot still slept in my bed at night, but I wondered how much longer I would have that pleasure.

We start to mourn our dogs before they leave us. Margot's rust-colored face had turned completely white, she had sprouted multiple warts, and her once-clear eyes became cloudy. By age sixteen she slept so soundly that I had to shake her awake. Arriving home after work, I would stand by her side and wait to hear her breathe, the interval between each inhale so long that I feared the worst. I had to stand her up to enable her to walk.

Quality of life issues are often subjective. Is it fair to keep a pet that can't see or hear, to put down a dog that can't walk outside except in a wagon or a baby carriage? Is it acceptable to assume that life is worth living because there is still a sliver of an appetite or an occasional spark of a life once lived? To love a pet means we bear witness to the full circle of life. We nurture and discipline, cherish and protect, but finally the most important part of loving, the part that completes the circle, is to let go, just as I did with Margot.

To this day, more than any other dog I've ever owned, Margot comes to me in my dreams. In my dream state, I imagine that she's been tucked away in my apartment, only somehow I've forgotten her. Sometimes she's sleeping comfortably in the curve of my body, radiating peaceful warmth. Other times she's running freely ahead of me, unaware of oncoming danger as she approaches an intersection. I rush to stop her. A look of surprise and fear spreads across her face as I scold her and then embrace her, relieved that she is safe. I love these nocturnal visits. Margot truly is the dog of my dreams.

49

IV   C O T T O N   I : In Hot Water

Ruben Beckermeyer stood behind the exam table, only his short red bangs and green eyes visible to me as I examined his dog. Having expressed a fear of needles, his mom waited in the lobby and his younger sister ricocheted around the exam room, pulling the hair out of her doll's head while babbling incessantly.

"Show me the needle," the redhead demanded.

My patient, a six-year-old bichon frisé, with a wavy white coat, drooping ears, and a curved tail was uncharacteristically frightened for her breed, and her human family was doing very little to comfort her.

"It's okay, Cotton. It won't hurt," I said right before I pierced her plump hip with the vaccine. She yipped and tried to get away. Ruben smiled with glee.

"It's all over, Mrs. Beckermeyer," I called through the door. "You can come in now." I offered Cotton a treat, which she ate quickly. "She may be sleepy from her shot today," I said.

"All she does is sleep anyway," said Ruben as they left.

Cotton Blossom Beckermeyer lived on Park Avenue, the pampered pet of a society psychiatrist, his wife, and their two children. Often confused with white poodles, bichon frisés gained popularity in New York for their adaptable, outgoing, and friendly personalities. Once the darlings of the Bourbon kings, they became the shipboard companions of Mediterranean pirates after falling out of favor with the court. By Cotton's time, they were fashionable with a different social set.

A canine status symbol, Cotton was purchased from Les Animeaux, a glitzy pet boutique on Madison Avenue. This high-end shop was owned by the notoriously famous Madame Patricia Florence, who managed to pass off puppy-mill pets as best-in-show material. Despite her relatively humble origins of Nebraska, Cotton had developed into a beautiful dog with a thick, tight, luxurious coat, and a perfect bite. I'd been told in confidence that Madame Florence often scolded herself for not having inflated Cotton's price even higher than she had. But the little dog turned out to be a healthy source of revenue for Madame Florence after all because Mrs. Beckermeyer had Cotton bathed weekly and her hair clipped every three weeks—such was her pride in her pet's appearance. Cotton's ever-expanding wardrobe of faux-Chanel sweaters, Louis Vuitton collars and leashes, stylish raincoats, the latest carrying bags, and other accessories were purchased from Les Animeaux, too.

Cotton ate designer pet foods, attended a dog gym, and frequented a dog day-care facility at least twice a week. Although afraid of water, she occasionally participated in aquatherapy sessions, the latest rage for Manhattan's upwardly mobile canine population. She was even enrolled in an agility class, where she was forced to navigate a maze of tunnels, bends, and jumps said to promote confidence and well being.

Mrs. Beckermeyer walked her dog once daily, when she took the children to school, relegating any other outdoor exercise to the housekeeper or the dog walker. If Mrs. Beckermeyer ever found green vomit on one of her Oriental rugs, the housekeeper was chastised for allowing Cotton to eat grass in Central Park. A more serious offense involved rolling in anything that smelled very, very good to Cotton and very, very bad to Mrs. Beckermeyer.

Sometimes, I would see Cotton in the park struggling against her finely tooled leather collar in an attempt to chase pigeons and squirrels. If she ate someone's discarded lunch, the food was unceremoniously removed from her mouth and she was reprimanded. She gazed longingly at other dogs running after tennis balls. Perhaps she had resigned herself to the fact that she would never be let off her leash, and harbored secret dreams to run wild and get into a little trouble.

As well-dressed, well-fed, and well-schooled as Ruben and his sister, Cotton was doted on, spoiled, and pampered. Although one might have thought that her canine instincts had been dulled as a result of the excesses bestowed upon her, in her heart she wanted the thing that all dogs crave—a deep, meaningful bond with her master. All she wanted was to love and be loved in return.

One Sunday evening, a message on my pager read, "*Cotton in hot water. Need advice. —Ann Beckermeyer.*" When I returned her call, Mrs. Beckermeyer told me that she'd been filling her bathtub that afternoon when Cotton had jumped or fallen into it. After the incident, Cotton had become very quiet, and she'd just now refused her dinner, which was quite unusual. I offered to meet them at the clinic but Mrs. Beckermeyer assured me that it wasn't an emergency. Besides, the family had just returned from their home in Connecticut and the kids still hadn't been put to bed. She was calling to make sure she could have an appointment first thing in the morning. I told her I would fit her in.

"Why," I asked myself, "would a six-year-old dog jump into a bathtub?"

In the examining room the next morning, it was obvious that Cotton's injuries were far worse than Mrs. Beckermeyer had reported. The little bichon's eyes were swollen closed and her lower chest and abdomen were shockingly red. Cotton's corneas were ulcerated, the superficial layer of cells were burned away, and her eyes absorbed the fluorescent dye placed in them, indicating extensive damage. "We'll have to keep her here," I said.

As the days unfolded, the extent of her injuries became more apparent. The fur on her chest and abdomen fell away, and then her oozing skin thickened and finally sloughed off.

She stood upright for hours, trembling, unable to endure the pain of lying on her stomach. With a yelp, she let us situate her so that she could sleep on her back. About 50 percent of the surface area of her body was seriously damaged. On several occasions, my staff and I discussed our reluctance to put Cotton through such a long and painful recovery. If she hadn't continued to eat everything we fed her, we would have ended her struggle. But Cotton persevered.

Gradually, her corneal ulcers healed, her skin turned from red to an almost ghostly white, and she could curl up and rest comfortably. Her ears had been so badly damaged that she lost much of the outer flaps, so when she was strong enough we surgically trimmed them into small, upright triangles, much like a schnauzer's ears. With her short ears and cropped coat, her large eyes seemed magnified. Once a hyper-groomed, dressed-to-kill glamour dog, Cotton now resembled a helpless Alaskan harbor seal cub.

We changed the dressings on her wounds, administered antibiotics to guard against infection, and held our breath. She was one of the most hopeless cases I had ever seen, but from the start she displayed a fierce hold on life and a gentle gratitude toward me and the other staff members who cared for her. We grew to respect her for her tremendous courage. She had to go it alone, without any love or attention from her family, who never once came to visit during her three-week recovery period.

Finally, it was time for Cotton to return home. But when Mrs. Beckermeyer found out that it would be necessary for her to change the dressings and clean the remaining

wounds, she asked that Cotton's stay be extended because
the household couldn't manage such tasks. Cotton was left
to languish in the hospital, where she had won the hearts of
everyone by virtue of her own brave heart. She had become
much more than a patient to me, and I liked to think that I
had become much more than a veterinarian to her. In her
previous visits, I had noted that she was an especially good
representative of her breed, but her courageous personality
had not yet won my attention. Now I had come to see her
character and her need.

I decided to take her home for the weekend. Even though I
lived about ten blocks from my clinic, I knew Cotton wouldn't
be up to the walk. Since it was rush hour and therefore
impossible to catch a cab, I decided to take her home on my
bicycle. I put her in a carrier with a zip-open top, strapped
her in securely, and pedaled home. She sniffed the air and
lifted her stubble-haired face to the breeze, effortlessly
handling the ride through the busy streets, and using her new
pointy ears to take in the jumble of noise. It appeared that my
patient was enjoying herself.

She was an easy houseguest and quickly found a place next
to my feet in bed. She ate well, was perfectly housebroken,
and was neither needy nor aloof. I was happy to make her
feel at home. The following week I phoned the Beckermeyers,
who put me off each day with a new excuse. I explained
that I wasn't doing anything for Cotton that they couldn't
do themselves, and insisted that it was time for her to rejoin
her family. They finally agreed to an appointment at 4:00 PM
on Friday to receive discharge instructions. But when Mrs.
Beckermeyer saw Cotton that afternoon, she turned away

with a little gasp, speechless. She was obviously horrified at the sight of her almost hairless, mostly earless dog, even as Cotton tried to lick her hands and nuzzle her head against her. "Please keep her for a few more days," she whispered. "I have to talk to my husband."

Dr. Beckermeyer was a talented psychopharmacologist so I was surprised that he had not been more proactive in Cotton's care and hospitalization. I was caught off guard when he asked me to speak to his son at the next discharge appointment. Ruben, his father explained, was suffering from a case of sibling rivalry that manifested itself in occasional rough play with Cotton. Dr. Beckermeyer hoped that I could explain Cotton's compromised medical situation and that her reentry into the home would occur without incident.

There was nothing I could do but take Cotton home with me for the weekend. When we arrived, she checked the corner of the kitchen where her food had been and pushed herself along the carpet, rubbing her face and shoulders against the rug. She was making herself at home. I chuckled out loud, pleased that she was so happy to be there.

When the next Friday rolled around, Ruben and Dr. Beckermeyer arrived at the appointed hour, and once again Cotton was obviously delighted to see her family, greeting them with tail wags and kisses. But she did act a little submissive as she greeted the boy.

"Ruben, you have a great dog," I told him. "She's been through so much and she's been a very brave girl. For a while, we didn't think she was going to make it. You're lucky she's able to go home with you. But you have to be gentle with her. Her skin is sensitive from her burns, so she needs a lot of rest and absolutely no roughhousing."

Ruben fingered the stethoscope on the exam table. I wasn't sure if I had his attention.

"Your job is to give her these pills twice daily in her food," I told him, "and put this cream on her earflaps three times a day." I hoped that by putting Ruben in charge of Cotton's care he would see her in a different, non-competitive light. "When you come back next week to get the stitches out of her ears, would you give me a report on how she's doing?"

"Uh-huh," he said, trying to listen to the sound of his own heartbeat with the stethoscope.

I suppose I should not have been surprised to receive Mrs. Beckermeyer's call a few days later. Cotton had bitten Ruben when he had "accidentally" pinched her ear while applying the medication. She swore it wasn't her son's fault, and thought it was time to put Cotton up for adoption. I told her to drop Cotton off at my office. I knew I had too much invested emotionally and professionally to consider placing her with a stranger or, worse, for the Beckermeyers to pursue "the other alternative."

Cotton was accustomed to a harried schedule and didn't mind the hectic, everyday craziness of our office. She befriended everyone, including Sunny and Berl, the office cats, and was fascinated by our parakeets, Celery and Parsley. She deepened her friendships with my staff and greeted the clients and patients at the door, earning the nickname Nurse

Cotton. To her delight, she was allowed to share a little food during our communal office lunch. Within two weeks she learned to follow us without getting in the way, and to stand behind the leaded screen when she heard the X-ray machine being turned on. She graduated from traveling in the carrier to riding in a wicker basket on my bicycle handlebars for our trip home on the weekends.

We posted a sign in the waiting room and made other inquiries, hoping to find an owner she could trust. Although a few people who were interested in bichon frisés came to inquire, there were no takers.

Although Cotton had been spayed, she was a very maternal dog. Whenever a litter of puppies or kittens came in, she became very excited, standing on her hind feet and sniffing the air like a miniature polar bear. She couldn't wait to check each one, licking them all over. We noticed that she loved children as well, for she always enthusiastically greeted those clients with carriages or strollers, and licked the occasional dangling baby foot or hand. She had a gentle way about her, and none of the mothers objected. I hoped that she would find a family with children again, as she seemed to have fond memories of them, despite her experience with the redhead.

Cotton lived at the hospital during the week and only came home with me on the weekends. Our weekends were so much fun that I didn't like the idea of her sleeping in her crate, alone, for the rest of the week. Every Monday night, as I prepared to leave her, she would fix her dark stare on me and lift her paws as I closed the office door behind me. It always broke my heart.

The second Monday in her adoption phase, Cotton had thrown up three times, probably from eating Berl's cat food. I stopped by to take a look at her before I left. I realized I could not leave her alone in the office that night, or any other night. It wasn't just that she needed a home; she needed me. I gave in to what had always been so obvious. We'd made the connection, and there was no going back. Cotton was now mine, and I was hers.

If we are lucky, we are allowed to share our lives with several dogs throughout our years. It's difficult to look back and decide which one affected you the most. Why does one stand out over all the others? Is it where you are in your own life that determines which one is your favorite, or are some dogs just so special, so extraordinary?

Cotton was to become the dog of my life.

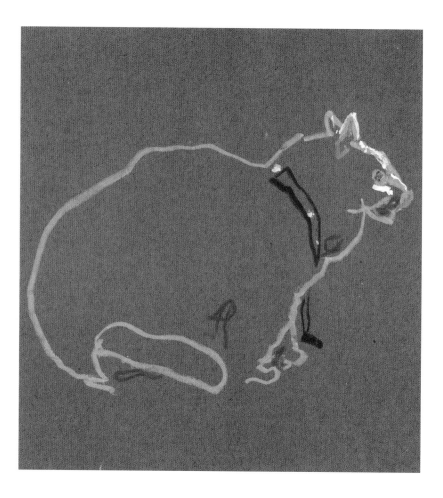

V R O W D Y : The March of Time

The first time we met, Mrs. MacMahon asked me to kill her cat. She placed her slightly dog-eared Louis Vuitton carrier on the exam table after refusing my offer to lift it for her. A dignified woman of indiscernible age, I later found out that she was a self-reliant widow and that her cat was her only companion.

"I think it's time," she said, looking directly into my eyes. "I don't want him to suffer." Then, leaning over the carrier, she cooed, "Come on out, Rowdy. Come and see the nice doctor." There was a lilt in her voice.

Rowdy was a male, domestic shorthair of a discernible age of seventeen years. His large frame, although somewhat depleted, indicated a sense of his former magnificence.

"You should have seen him, doctor, a few years ago. He was the most handsome cat I've ever owned. But look at him now. He's dropped so much weight. I'm sure it's his time."

The cat sat sphinx-like on the table as he took in the sights and smells around him. He seemed amused to be out of the house and on an outing. Certainly, he was relaxed as he observed me without a trace of apprehension. A large red tabby with round, somewhat faded green eyes, he shared the coloring of his mistress. It was obvious that she'd been an auburn beauty in her time. Her no-nonsense demeanor suggested that she was perhaps unaware that she was still an attractive woman. A keen light radiated from her green eyes. Perhaps it's true, I mused to myself, that with time owners and their pets begin to resemble one another.

"Your cat still has a lot of spirit left in him," I said after I finished a cursory examination. "Why don't you let me run a few tests and see if we can help him?"

"Do you really think you can?" she beamed. Her mood shifted noticeably and she became talkative. She told me that her husband had rescued Rowdy as a kitten from a trash can during a raging snowstorm. She'd be so happy if she could have him a bit longer. Her children had moved out of state, and although she visited them and they had offered her a place with them, New York City was her home. She confided that her daughter-in-law didn't really like cats.

"I'm too old to be a nanny," she added. Then she looked at Rowdy and said, "But you're never too old to be needed."

Rowdy's blood tests were mostly normal, although he did have slightly elevated kidney-function levels. We sent him home on a low-protein diet and I warned Mrs. MacMahon that someday she might need to give her cat injections of fluid underneath his skin to aid his failing kidneys.

"I wouldn't want him to suffer," she said. We scheduled a follow-up appointment and she left with a spring in her step.

"Doctor, you're a miracle worker," she exclaimed when I saw her a month later. "He's been eating better and drinking less and meeting me at the door again when I come home from the market. He hasn't done that in ages." She radiated cheer as she coaxed Rowdy from his carrier, and to my eye the mistress looked more improved than the patient. Rowdy apparently felt better on his new diet, but it was not enough to stem the march of time against his aging kidneys. His kidney function had deteriorated to the point that I thought it would be necessary to give him fluids by injection on a daily basis.

Once again, Mrs. MacMahon made it clear that she did not want Rowdy to suffer. I assured her that many owners within my practice gave their cats injections daily, and that the procedure was fast and relatively painless. She agreed to try the regimen but insisted that she would stop if it made Rowdy uncomfortable in any way. She confided that she had handled injections during her husband's long and fatal illness.

"Suffering's for saints and martyrs," she said, "not for God's little creatures."

On her return visit several months later, Mrs. MacMahon once again announced that she was sure it was Rowdy's time. He was refusing his special diet, had lost weight, and was drinking more water. Occasionally, he even vomited. Not only that, but he refused the steamed cod she made and wouldn't eat the bits of cantaloupe that had always been his favorite.

With his fur and skin now too ample for his shrinking bulk, Rowdy appeared to be wearing an oversized coat. He sat on the exam table staring blankly ahead, the light all but extinguished from his sunken green eyes.

Mrs. MacMahon also seemed faded, but as ever she was focused. "I'll want his ashes back in an urn," she said to me with determination in her voice and posture. "I'll feel better when he's back at home with me."

I agreed that now it was time to help Rowdy out of this world. As his owner bent to sign the consent form, a single tear splashed onto the exam table. When she looked up, I could see that the light had gone out of her eyes, too. She looked directly at me and said, "I'm ready."

Folded in his owner's arms, Rowdy passed on peacefully, the transition from life smooth and seamless. "He needed that," she said. "There was no fight left in him." Touching her hand in an acknowledgment of her pain, I left them in the room to have a moment together.

* * *

One afternoon several months later, I was on my way to a doctor's appointment of my own on a sunny, warm mid-October day. I could hear the hum of cars as they raced across the river on the Triborough Bridge. Climbing the steep hill where York Avenue rises beyond Fifty-ninth Street to become Sutton Place, I noticed Mrs. MacMahon walking toward me in sensible shoes, square-shouldered and with an athletic stride. Smiling in recognition, she asked me, "What are you doing in my neck of the woods, doctor?" As I answered her I noted that the color had returned to her complexion and the sparkle was back in her eyes.

"And how are you getting along?" I asked.

She looked away for a moment, running her fingers through her hair to tuck in an errant wisp. "It was pretty tough at first. I couldn't believe that Rowdy was gone. I saw him everywhere, and I missed him terribly."

"I'm so sorry," I lamely replied as she went on.

"I slept with that cat every night for seventeen years. He followed me everywhere I went, and just knowing he was there was a comfort for me. You know, doctor, in a way it was worse than when I lost my husband."

"I'm so sorry," I repeated. I'd often heard that grief for a pet could be as profound as that for a family member.

"At least when my husband died, he left me some money." She winked as we shared a laugh and then went on our respective ways.

VI MATISSE AND RENAULT:
A Cat Lover's Collection

The new client sat in the well-worn leather wing chair, cradling Cotton in her lap. She chirped, "What a pretty dog," in a distinct New York accent. She was so caught up in her affectionate display that Ro, my receptionist, had to raise her voice to ask her to step into the exam room. Cotton seemed smitten and followed her.

She introduced herself in a voice that was deep and distinctive. "I am Sally Ganz." Short, silver-haired, and petite, she hoisted her carrier onto the table, smiled, and firmly shook my hand.

"This is Matisse. He is the most independent cat I have ever owned," she rasped as she leaned against the exam table, which hid three-fourths of her body.

Once out of the carrier, her cat, a young sable Burmese, looked around eagerly, ready to jump off the exam table and explore the room. As we discussed the different types of feline personalities (highly social, love-starved, aloof, et cetera.), I examined Matisse. The cat gave off a rich, nutty tobacco scent as I approached his ears with my otoscope, my nose only inches from his face. I could always tell the smokers from the non-smokers just by holding their pets.

Mrs. Ganz, dressed in khaki slacks and a man-tailored white, starched.shirt told me that she'd bring in her second cat, Renault, to see me the next week. We talked some more as I gave Matisse his vaccination, and Mrs. Ganz filled the room with her moderated New Yorkese. Then, fingering a long strand of what were probably costume pearls, she asked if we'd be finished soon as she had a doctor's appointment of her own.

"We're finished now," I said as I discarded the needle syringe into the red plastic sharps container. "It was a pleasure to meet you," I told her, and I meant it, having enjoyed her spunky demeanor and certain "no nonsense" charm. I wrote up her record card and gave her the usual 10 percent senior citizen discount.

*   *   *

Two weeks after our first meeting, Mrs. Ganz paid a second visit with Renault, her voice even deeper than I remembered. She greeted me with a hug, as if we were old friends, exclaiming, "Isn't he gorgeous?!" After introducing me to Renault, she explained that, unlike her other cat, Matisse, Renault followed her from room to room, slept on her bed, and was a source of great joy. He was a sweet and affable cat, curious and poised. He head-butted my arm as I looked him over, and purred so loudly I couldn't auscultate his heart properly.

This time Mrs. Ganz sat and watched as my assistant Audra held Renault for the injection, a proud smile of ownership playing across her face. Once again I noticed a strong scent of tobacco, but knew this might just as easily have come from Audra, who took several cigarette breaks a day outside the office, rain or shine.

The exam finished, Mrs. Ganz cleared her throat several times as she rose from the chair. As we said good-bye, she looked even smaller than I remembered. I told her I'd see her next year for her cats' annual check ups, and wished her happy holidays.

Several days before Christmas, the office activity slowed as people left town or rushed to finish holiday chores. I took advantage of the lull in my schedule to run to a nearby shop, hoping to pick up something extra for the office gift exchange. As I was choosing a few small items, I spotted a sweater I wanted to give to my niece. I needed to speak to a salesperson about sizes, so I approached the store clerk for help. As the clerk turned to address me I was surprised to see that this gray-haired senior was, in fact, Mrs. Ganz. Since she wasn't carrying a coat or handbag I assumed she was supplementing her social security or pension as a temporary holiday worker paid in part on commission.

"I do not work here, doctor," she said, each word a small pebble in her gravel-voiced explanation. "I am shopping for my grandchildren. My car and driver are waiting for me outside." So that clarified things and explained why she didn't bother to carry a jacket or a sweater on this blustery winter day. I suddenly became overwhelmingly warm as my face flushed and my ears reddened at the thought of the miscalculation I'd made of my client's situation. Once again we parted with an exchange of holiday wishes.

On my way back to the office, I passed the Metropolitan Museum of Art and noticed several large banner flags advertising the museum's current exhibits. One of them proudly boasted the collection of Victor and Sally Ganz. Apparently, my client didn't need the 10 percent senior citizen discount I had been giving her; she owned one of the largest and most revered collections of modern art in America.

* * *

The new year started with a call from Mrs. Ganz. Her voice deeper than ever, she rasped into the phone that she was ill, bed-ridden, and taking medication that she assumed made her unattractive to both of her cats. Her beloved Renault would no longer approach her. I told her how sorry I was to hear she wasn't feeling well and she assured me that she would be up and out of bed soon. I assumed that she was still smoking as our conversation was occasionally interrupted by paroxysms of coughing. Although I knew of nothing medical she could do to make her cats more responsive, I recommended that she place some catnip toys around her bed and playfully suggested that she anoint herself with oil from a can of tuna fish, an idea she accepted with great humor. Her throaty laughter filled my ear and was quickly followed by a long, laborious coughing jag.

I never knew if she tried the tuna trick or if it worked if she did. Several weeks later I read her obituary in the New York Times, a lengthy piece about her respected art collection and her generous philanthropy. Renault and Matisse were to live with a family member upstate.

I had only met Mrs. Ganz three times, but will always remember her easy smile, her lack of pretension, and the great joy she found in our common denominator, her two cats.

VII   E M M A N Y : Diamond Dog

Mrs. Taylor and her family had just returned from the Christmas-tree-lighting ceremony on Park Avenue. Up and down the avenue, tall Norway spruces adorned each corner of the rectangular islands that divided the traffic on the wide street. In the spring, swathes of tulips would gracefully brighten the corners; in summer, impatiens. But the effect of more than one hundred majestic trees covered in miniature lights lining Park Avenue like sentinels was the most dazzling spectacle. Every year, Laura, Tom, and their two daughters joined their neighbors and fellow Junior-Leaguers as the trees were lit with great fanfare and Christmas caroling. One particular afternoon, New York City had been hit by a record-setting blizzard, so the lighting ceremony was even more dramatic and spectacular than usual.

"Emmany, Emmany!" Laura called as she entered her foyer, waiting for the enthusiastic greeting she received from her beloved dog whenever she returned home. Emmany, a sixteen-month-old ruby-colored Cavalier King Charles spaniel that Laura had imported from England, had never disappointed her before. That night, however, she was nowhere to be seen. "Where's Emmany?" Laura asked.

"She's in here, honey," Tom said. He had found Emmany in their bedroom, where the young dog had managed to spill the contents of an ormolu jewelry box from the dressing table. The spaniel sat among an impressive trove of glittering stones and wagged her tail as she cast her liquid-brown eyes up at her mistress. "Emmany, what have you done?" gasped Laura.

I left the clinic early that day, as most of my afternoon clients had cancelled due to the storm. I carried Cotton home through the drifting snow, admiring New York City all dressed up for Christmas. As I entered my apartment building, my pager vibrated. The message read, *"Call Laura Taylor. Dog swallowed diamond. Worried about Emmany. Wants ring back also."*

Dogs and cats manage to swallow a lot of peculiar things. I've surgically removed ribbons, coins, and even a telephone cord from patients. Dogs frequently ingest bones, stones, staples, and other sharp objects. Cats favor rubber bands, thread, and dental floss, and they seem to especially enjoy digesting cooking twine. A swallow of peroxide could induce vomiting if a pet swallowed pills, chocolate, or some poisonous materials, but not everything can be regurgitated. Sharp or jagged objects could be more harmful when vomited than when passed. With many foreign objects, it's a wait-and-watch situation. Remembering that Mrs. Taylor's ring was unusually large, I feared that vomiting might cause Emmany esophageal damage. We would have to watch and wait.

At 1010 Park Avenue that evening, there was an air of anxiety. Laura's six-carat, pear-shaped, flawless diamond ring had been in Tom's family for generations, and Laura had received it by default. Tom's older brother had given it to his first fiancée, but then was left standing alone at the altar. After a lengthy legal battle, the ring came back into his possession at the same time Tom and Laura were engaged. Now the ring rarely left Laura's finger, and she cursed her fate that she hadn't worn it that evening. Not only did it have a great deal of sentimental value, but she also enjoyed the ring's luster and the unspoken envy it evoked. But the blizzard had persuaded her to slip off the ring so that she could wear her tight-fitting Bottega Veneta cashmere-lined ostrich leather gloves to the tree-lighting ceremony.

Tom, who hadn't noticed that Laura wasn't wearing her diamond, was unaware that it was missing. Laura had called quietly from the bathroom to leave her desperate message and hoped to somehow retrieve the ring before anyone realized it was lost.

To make matters worse, Tom's now-married older brother and his wife had been invited for cocktails that evening, and the four of them were then going out to dinner. The story of the much-coveted ring inevitably wound its way into the conversation whenever the two couples were together, and the new sister-in-law always asked to try it on. Her own diamond was quite respectable, but no match for the heirloom that would have been hers had Tom not proposed to Laura at that particular moment in time. Laura panicked at the thought of

having to admit that the diamond the Taylor family had nearly lost fourteen years ago was, for the moment at least, nowhere to be found.

She *had* to get the ring back.

When I returned the emergency page, Laura answered the phone on the first ring.

"No, it's not life threatening," I said. "It will probably pass in a day or two. Please call me if Emmany stops eating or is sick to her stomach."

Laura usually left the job of walking Emmany to her children or to her housekeeper, and Tom walked the dog at night. Laura enjoyed lavishing attention on Emmany, but she hated the New York City law that required an owner to pick up the dog's excrement. She couldn't, however, ask Emmany's walker to bring home the contents of the plastic bag without revealing that she had lost the treasured ring. Even if Loyola, the housekeeper, were willing to search for the missing jewel after each walk—something Laura couldn't bring herself to request—once she knew of the valuable loss, could Loyola be trusted? No, if Emmany had eaten the ring, Laura knew she would have to walk and clean up after the spaniel herself.

Her mind churning, Laura realized that in order to search for the ring she would not only have to walk Emmany four times a day, but would have to return with her plastic bag to the apartment. This would entail passing the doorman and riding up the elevator manned by the chatty, white-gloved operator—not to mention the neighbors. She would have to find a way to disguise the plastic bag and its contents.

Grabbing her Coach pocketbook that matched Emmany's leash, collar, and coat—a "gift" from the dog on Mother's Day—Laura announced, "Tom, I'm taking Emmany out for her walk. I don't mind, really. It's so pretty outside." The elevator operator commented on the fierceness of the storm and the doorman warned her to be careful of the ice.

As they made their way along the avenue, Laura talked to Emmany. "Are you okay, sweetie?" she asked, trying to judge each nuance of Emmany's facial expressions and body language. It was difficult to scold her. "How could you do such a thing?" she asked. The little dog wagged her tail and pulled her owner down the street. After a walk around the block with no results, Laura gave up and returned to face the arrival of her in-laws.

At 8:00 PM the doorman announced the arrival of Tom's older brother, Thaddeus, and his wife, Elyssa. After warm greetings all around, the children were sent to bed and Tom offered cosmopolitans to the ladies while he and Thaddeus enjoyed triple-malt Scotch. He also served hors d'oeuvres at his wife's request. Laura did not want her hands to be visible as the grilled monkfish liver with white truffle paste was passed around. Emmany eyed the tray of food from her comfortable perch on a down-filled ottoman near the fire. The fried oyster mushrooms with reduced coconut milk were a potent lure as well. Laura kept her left hand in the pocket of her Prada pants.

"I just love this weather," declared Elyssa. "We never see snow like this down home in Buckhead. I love the way those Christmas trees look with the lights and snow, all up and down the avenue—so elegant. Let's go to the window and have a look."

It only took a moment for Emmany to leave her spot by the fire and gobble up what was left of the repast—monkfish liver, oyster mushrooms, and the leftover marinated beef with mango horseradish.

"Emmany! What have you done now?" cried Laura, who tried to imagine how this would play into the saga of the missing ring.

"Don't worry about her, honey. We're going to be late," said Tom.

Mortimer's restaurant was abuzz with pre-holiday merriment, and the couples were seated at Tom and Laura's favorite table. Laura ordered the chicken potpie since she could eat it without a knife. Her left hand sat in her lap as she repeatedly thumbed the vacant area on her wedding finger.

"Laura, you're so quiet. Are you okay?" asked Elyssa.

"I'm fine. I'm just a little worried about Emmany. I'm afraid she's going to be sick from all those things she's eaten." After dinner, the foursome returned to Tom and Laura's home for nightcaps.

When the elevator door opened on to the marble foyer of their home, Emmany was conspicuously absent. Calling out the spaniel's name, Laura hurried from room to room. She entered the guest room and her search was interrupted by the sight and smell of several little mounds of vomit scattered on the Aubusson rug and a lumpy pile in the center of the monogrammed Porthault comforter.

"Emmany, are you in here? Are you okay?" Laura cooed to her spaniel, who didn't respond. Retrieving a hand towel from the guest bathroom, she began to clean the mess on the bed. That's when she felt something hard within the soft contents.

"Laura, is everything okay?" called Elyssa, coming down the hall. "Have you found her?"

"Everything's just fine," Laura gagged, summoning the courage to slide the slippery jewel on her finger. Emmany popped her head out from under the bed.

"Laura, you should take that ring off before you clean up that mess," said Elyssa. "Oh, my. I think that comforter is ruined."

"Honey, I know it is," smiled Laura, wondering if it was the beef mango or fish truffle combination that was responsible for Emmany's upset stomach and her own good fortune. "I'm going to call the vet."

Cotton and I were on our evening walk. The snow had been falling heavily and the streets were largely deserted. We watched giant flakes swirled around the city streetlights as we plunged through the drifts. Feeling the familiar vibration of my pager, I pulled it out of my pocket and read: *"Laura Taylor called. Cancel last message. Got ring back. Emmany fine, too."*

VIII   C H A M P : Saint Francis and the Orphans

George and Mary Cutrone were an older Italian couple who owned a bodega in Spanish Harlem in New York City. George was the sort of guy who extended credit to customers who could never pay him back, and he had a reputation for taking in stray cats or dogs—*orfani* (orphans), he called them. For this Mary scolded him, teasingly calling him Saint George. Yet she was the one who regularly trapped skinny stray cats in the backyards of shabby New York City tenements, brought them home, and gave them *cosa di mangiare* (something to eat). Not long after they moved there, the Cutrone's store became a drop-off point for many of the homeless animals found in the neighborhood. Cotton was always very happy to get *cosa di mangiare* from the Cutrones when they visited the clinic.

George immigrated to the United States from Tuscany just after the Second World War. The oldest of six brothers and sisters, he moved to America with the hopes of opening a delicatessen in order to earn enough money to help his siblings back home. His ultimate goal was to reach San Francisco and the wine country where his fellow *paisani* had flocked. The California climate and topography resembled their homeland, but was without the poverty and desolation that had rocked post-war Italy.

George had stopped in New York City on his way to California to visit a newly immigrated friend when he met Mary Fontana, the American-born daughter of an Italian brickmaker, at the Toscano Club in Brooklyn. Mary volunteered as a hostess at the club and sometimes entertained at the piano singing patriotic Italian songs. George described this meeting with Mary as a *colpa di fulmine* (a lightning strike), for he was instantly smitten.

After they were married, they settled in New York City and opened a bodega on East 116th Street in Spanish Harlem. They hoped to have a large family, but weren't blessed that way. Mary had always envied the large, boisterous, and seemingly happy families of her *zii* and *zie* (aunts and uncles), and so she directed her maternal energy to those young nieces and nephews.

Their first stray dog was a large mixed-breed female that Mary coaxed off the train tracks at Grand Central Station. The pregnant dog soon gave birth to eight puppies. It broke her heart to part with any of the pups, but she did place all but one in homes around the neighborhood. Her prize from this litter, a snow-white male called Alba, resembled a German shepherd and accompanied her everywhere, greeting the customers and guarding the bodega in the days before health inspectors regularly slapped "No Dogs Allowed" signs on store windows. Through the years, George and Mary prospered. Their store, La Speranza (The Hope), generated a steady income that enabled them to continue their generosity toward animals as well as toward some not-so-well-off customers. Their *famiglia*, as George referred to the pets, became too numerous to count, and usually hovered anywhere from between twenty to thirty cats, not to mention a rotating roster of various dogs. The cats lived in the Cutrones' apartment and in the bodega's basement. The exact number of animals fluctuated whenever some of them were lucky enough to get adopted.

I first met the Cutrones when I was a young intern at a clinic on Seventy-sixth Street and Fifth Avenue. This was probably the most expensive vet office in New York City and the Cutrones stood out among the Fifth Avenue clientele. Their ragtag mixed breeds and backyard cats were a far cry from the sculpted poodles and sleek purebreds that typically filled the waiting room. But the Cutrones believed they were getting the best care for their animals because they were paying so much for each visit. When I opened my own practice on the East side, the Cutrones were my first clients, and the small statue of Saint Francis they gave me back then still stands above a cabinet in my exam room. George and Mary often came to the office with two or three orphans at a time. My receptionist, Ro, brought me a chart that indicated the breed (always "mixed"), age (always "in question"), and gender.

Unfortunately, with so many orphans it was impossible to give them individual attention or for George and Mary to remember each one's name, if it had even received a name. But the important thing was that the cats were off the street, fed, vaccinated, and out of harm's way as they waited to find a permanent home. Our conversations often repeated themselves and usually began with me asking, "What's this one's name, Mary?"

"*Non lo so.* I have so many, I can't remember."

"But, Mary, we need a name for the files. You've got too many black-and-white cats for me to tell one from the other."

"Then call him Micio," she would say. I knew that *micio* meant "pussycat."

"But, Mary, you called the last one Micio. Today is Tuesday, so let's call this one Tuesday. Next week is Christmas, so how about Nicholas for the boy?" "Whatever you say," answered Mary in her slightly broken English. "It is hard enough to feed and clean up after them all, yet alone name them."

At Easter, we named a pit bull mix Pasqua, and an all-white domestic short-haired kitten Bunny. The Fourth of July brought Paul Revere, a Chihuahua with a missing tail. Valentino, an ancient old pug, was christened on Valentine's Day. My favorite, though, was Money, a beagle mix that the Cutrones picked up on April 15, income tax day. George liked to recount the time he ran through the streets of Spanish Harlem yelling, "Money!" when the dog had slipped out of its collar and run away.

On a particularly busy Saturday morning, Ro interrupted an exam to tell me that Mary was on the phone with an emergency. She was coming with Champ, who was really sick, and wanted to see me as soon as she got to the office. I agreed, remembering Champ, a one-hundred-pound-plus Rottweiler,

who more accurately should have been named Killer. We had to muzzle or sedate him during each visit.

The waiting room was jammed with anxious pets and their owners when the front entrance door swung open as the Cutrones and two strangers struggled to carry Champ past the astonished onlookers.

"Come right into the exam room," I said, aware at first glance that the emergency was over. Champ was quiet, too quiet, and the form they carried through my busy waiting room was already in rigor mortis.

"Can you help him?" Mary asked, out of breath, her apron covered with fur.

"Can't you do anything for him?" pleaded George at her side, his shirt soaked in sweat from his efforts.

"Mary, *mi dispiace*," I stammered. It was surprisingly difficult to say what was obvious. "Champ is gone. It's too late," I said, tugging on one of his immovable limbs. "He has passed on."

"But his eyes are open," she said, unwilling to accept the truth. "He doesn't feel cold."

"I'm sorry, Mary. There's nothing anyone can do. He's dead."

They departed in tears.

The sight of Champ being carried through the waiting room was sure to have reminded each of my other clients of the mortality of their own pets. I wondered if they would think I had failed Champ in some way. Would I have to re-establish trust with each of them?

My next patient was a Siamese kitten to be vaccinated. "Doc, that last one looked pretty bad," the client said. "Are you going to be able to help him?"

And so it went the rest of the morning. I had to explain to each of those who had seen Champ that he had died several hours before he arrived at the clinic. Part of the commitment to a puppy or a kitten is the knowledge that we will one day have to say good-bye.

It wasn't long before Mary brought in her latest find, a middle-aged graying boxer with uncropped ears scarred by time spent on the street.

"Mary, what should we call this one?" I asked her.

She smiled. She had anticipated my question. "I call him Champ. After all, he's a boxer and it's a name I'll never forget."

George and Mary eventually closed the bodega, but they still live in the apartment above the store. The stairs are tough on Mary's arthritis. It wouldn't matter much if their animals had names because George has a hard time remembering much of anything now. A crooked smile appears on Mary's face as she playfully calls their time together their "golden years."

They now have one dog, a collie-shepherd mix named Pearl and two shy almost feral cats that live under the bed in another bedroom. George faithfully walks Pearl three times a day. The two of them are a familiar sight in the neighborhood: the tall, spare *anziano* (old one) with his thin, angular, graying companion. George and Mary are greeted affectionately by the many neighbors whose lives they touched with their generosity to the community and its animals.

They talk about retiring to Florida, and sometimes George ruefully suggests California. But they have no friends there, and they think the change would be hard on Pearl and the cats. If they have any regrets about their lives, or how little they have now, they've never mentioned it to me.

I wonder what will become of them as they grow older. I hope that the plastic Saint Francis statue above my cabinet has enough power to help those who help the animals, as well as the animals themselves.

IX L O G A N : Design for Life

The children were too young to take the passing of Logan seriously, but it was an event of great magnitude in Leith Peabody's life.

Nineteen years earlier, when she had first arrived in New York City ready to decorate the world or at least the Northeastern Seaboard, she adopted Logan from a client who was allergic to cats. The four-month-old Scottish Fold had symmetrical black-and-white markings and an inherent dignity that appealed to Leith's sense of beauty and order. Before long, Leith's attention to detail and design savvy led her to the august firm of Boggs and Bailey. She became known as one of the famous designers of the day, and her work was featured in magazines that showcased the homes of the rich and famous. Logan, too, gained notoriety as the cat cradled in Leith's arms in several of the photographs, which appeared in magazines and books, year after year.

Logan developed into a magnificent specimen of his breed. His ears, folded in half and cub-like, were exactly as a Scottish Fold's ears should be. His black coat shone in contrast to his white face, chest, and paws. A perfect green-eyed tuxedo cat, he always sported a Scottish plaid ribbon around his neck, a motif found consistently in Leith's work.

Her career and her cat meant everything to Leith, and as she adjusted to the likelihood that this would be enough to keep her happy, she met and married Walker Hawkins. He not only shared Leith's enthusiasm for her work and success, but he understood the place that Logan occupied in her life. Never having had pets himself, he grew to love Logan with a fierceness that rivaled, but could never match, Leith's.

Leith thought life could be no sweeter, until the addition of their twin daughters, Ashley and Aubrey, proved her wrong. But Leith's first love would always be Logan. She loved him unswervingly. They had a history together. He had shared the small studio apartment with Leith on the Upper East Side. There, Leith had laid black-and-white tile in the tiny foyer to coordinate with the colors of Logan's luxurious coat. The remnants of satin plaid that trimmed the throw pillows of her sofa were used to cover the cushions of Logan's basket bed. It's possible that New Yorkers bond so closely with their pets because, unlike people upstate or in the Midwest or even in New Jersey, they share uncommonly tight spaces. In every way, Leith and Logan had been and still were inseparable.

Over the years together, Leith and Logan had come to enjoy an unspoken language. Leith could interpret the subtle nuances of Logan's eye movements and what the different positions and speed of his tail twitches meant. Logan, for his part, had been a fairly good sport about the changes that time had wrought. It had been his good fortune to move from their small studio apartment where he would sun in a small flower box on the windowsill to a large apartment where he patrolled the lushly planted wraparound terrace and occasionally snagged an errant pigeon.

His devotion to Leith was unshakable, yet he accepted Walker and recognized that the twins were part and parcel of his beloved mistress.When cornered by the precocious toddlers, he might have thrown a claws-retracted feline punch, but he never considered using his teeth. He romped with the children by day but shared the bed with Leith and Walker by night, curled up at foot's end on Leith's side. As the girls grew, he learned when to approach them for affection, and when to retreat to the granite countertops in the kitchen for safety.

When Ashley and Aubrey started nursery school, Leith noticed that Logan looked a bit thinner. Although his appetite was better than usual, his skin seemed too large for his frame and he was drinking more water than usual. Logan was diagnosed as hyperthyroid, a common condition of older cats. Since he was too old for surgery or radioactive iodine treatment, he began taking medication twice a day. Then, at age nineteen, Logan stopped eating, and he could no longer jump onto the bed. To ease the suffering associated with renal failure, Leith learned how to administer fluids under Logan's skin. But the day finally came when it was obvious that there was little quality left in Logan's life.

Leith made a noon appointment, aware that the waiting room would be quiet and empty for the lunch hour. She would give Logan two milligrams of Valium one hour before arriving at the clinic. It was important that the procedure go smoothly and be performed with great dignity.

Leith arrived on time, her large, dark sunglasses hiding her puffy face. The cat carrier was strewn with rose petals and laced with catnip. Walker and the twins were waiting in the car. It was his job to explain what Mommy had to do, and to prepare them for the loss of a friend who had always been there.

I instructed Ro to hold all calls and then prepared a dose of anesthesia as well as a dose of concentrated barbiturate to help Logan out of this world as gently as possible. With an almost imperceptible nod from Leith, I administered the intravenous injection that induced sleep, and then a second injection that pushed Logan into the beyond. Leith requested a lock of his hair, and removed the ever-present ribbon. Tears streaming from behind the dark lenses, she silently embraced me and then was gone.

Standing there alone with Logan, I felt a huge sense of sadness. I had known them both for such a long time. Leith had always been a caring client. Logan had always been a charming patient. They were my friends. As I held Logan's lifeless body, I remembered moving to New York with my dog Margot. She'd been sixteen when I made the agonizing decision to put her down. I had administered the injections myself. At moments like this, I experienced an old and profound feeling of grief.

Leith had requested that we hold Logan until Friday when the family would bury Logan on Sagaponac, Long Island, but the untimely arrival of a double case of mumps kept the family from their usual weekend pilgrimage. Leith telephoned and asked me to keep Logan for another week. Cringing at the delicacy of the situation, I nevertheless told her that I would have to move Logan from the refrigerator to the freezer. We agreed that nothing else could be done and made arrangements for the following Friday.

When the Hawkins arrived the following week, they were once again a happy family. The twins had been industrious during their recuperation and were carrying an obviously handmade wooden box.

"We made this for Logan," explained Ashley. Leith had decided to turn Logan's burial into a family affair. The box, a narrow rectangle, was decorated with drawings of various animals, especially cats as well as kids, clouds, and crucifixes. The children seemed gleeful at the prospect of the funeral service to come and Leith, ever the good mom, was able to suppress her pain and her personal preferences regarding Logan's final arrangements in order to guide her children through one of life's most difficult lessons.

Walker handed me the funeral box and I went to get Logan from his temporary resting place in the freezer. He had been placed head-to-tail in a natural sleeping position and was now a solid, circular mass. Sizing up the situation, I could see that I had a problem. No matter how I tried, it was obvious that Logan, in his frozen form, would not fit in the box. Trying to explain this to the family and maintain the dignity of the situation might be even more difficult. I asked Ro to send Leith into my exam room.

"I don't know how to say this delicately, so I'm just going to be direct. Logan's body is frozen and in his current position won't fit into the little box."

"Oh, my," murmured Leith. "I didn't want the children to actually see Logan. I thought we'd just drive him out to the country and bury him. How long do you think it would take for—"

"—About twelve hours," I interrupted, sparing her from uttering the word "defrost" that all but hung in the air. There was nothing we could do but wait.

* * *

The white garden at the Hawkins House, a converted potato barn in Sagaponac, was as perfect as any of those shown in the magazines in which Leith's work was so often featured. A gate gave way to a meandering path, a swath of grass maintained like a putting green and lined in the spring with crowds of white tulips and lilies-of-the-valley. Past a rippling bed of fragrant white lavender, there was a pergola where Leith often sat. From this corner of the garden, set off by mounds of white phlox, Casablanca lilies, and an almost-out-of-control bed of catnip, one could see a small marker of carrera marble. On closer inspection, the inscription read:

Here lies Logan, 1977–1996

Boon Companion to Ashley and Aubrey

Faithful Friend to Walker

We Shared So Much

All Things Pass But Nothing Is Forgotten

X C O T T O N I I: Redemption

Cotton and I became a familiar sight in our Manhattan neighborhood. We rode back and forth to work on my bicycle. People often noticed the little pointy-eared bichon frisé sitting in her wicker basket with what could be interpreted as a smile on her face. As I maneuvered through the city streets, Cotton observed the dogs we passed as she leaned into the turns.

I talked to Cotton a lot. She had lived with a family, and although she had plenty of stimulation each day at the office, I didn't want her to feel bored in her new home. I would comment on the weather or ask her opinion about a song. In the mornings, I would wake up and tell her I had slept well. She would cock her head toward me and gaze with rapt attention, trying to interpret what I meant. One morning, about a block from the office, we passed a homeless man pushing a dog in a shopping cart. The man was dressed in a multicolored coat and the dog also wore a colored coat.

"Cotton," I said, as we pulled up to the office door, "did you see what I saw?" I was feeling less than charitable that day as I secretly hoped that this particular homeless man and his dog were not on their way to my office. At the office, I had begun making my rounds of the patients when Ro alerted me to a walk-in appointment. Her voice had a get-a-load-of-this tone to it. I entered the exam room and the homeless man and his puppy were waiting for me, a shopping cart stationed next to them. Thinking that some of my Upper East Side clients would be put off by my newest client and his pet, I decided to hurry through the exam before the office began to get busy.

Ro handed me the chart and I noticed that the lines for the address and telephone number were blank. My client, whose name was James, was in his early thirties and was handsome in a scruffy way with a full beard and shoulder-length brown hair parted down the middle. He had startlingly light blue, deep-set eyes and he spoke articulately. My patient, Suzy, was a six-month-old Labrador retriever mix. She kept her eyes fixed adoringly on him and never stopped wagging her tail.

Their coats were truly remarkable handmade garments. James, I discovered, collected broken umbrellas ruined by the gusty city winds and his long overcoat was patched with the recycled material. Robe-like and belted at the waist with a braided rope, the coat fell in several colorful folds to the floor, and evoked the garb of Saint Francis whose statue peered down from the cabinet above us. I noticed a Burberry logo among the several sewn patches of waterproof fabric and plastic bags Suzy sported on her back. This colorful coat kept the wind, rain, and cold of the city streets at bay, a necessity since the pair usually slept on a subway grate outside of Bloomingdale's. Dogs were not permitted in the homeless shelters.

The shopping cart was neatly piled high with all of their possessions. There was a twenty-pound bag of Puppy Chow as well as several gallons of bottled water. A rolled sleeping bag was tied to one side of the cart and a plastic bag filled with bottles and cans was tied to the other side. There were various articles of folded clothing, a rusted pair of dumbbells, and a coiled jump rope. A solitary hairbrush hung from the handle of the cart. I wondered if they shared it.

Inside the cart, a stack of hardbound books revealed James's interest in Hermann Hesse. Tied beneath the handles of the cart, covering the *Thank You for Shopping Gristedes* sign, were a pair of polished Cordovan leather penny loafers, even though the shoes James wore were old sneakers held together with silver duct tape.

James told me that Suzy hadn't had her shots. Suzy had found James sleeping near the Central Park boat basin. He had been roused from his slumber by the sound of Suzy chewing through a Styrofoam container of food that James had found for his own dinner. He named her Suzy because her eyes were as dark as black-eyed Susans. He kept her because she was even less well off than he was. She was about three months old at the time and they had been together ever since.

Without a vaccination, Suzy was at risk of getting parvovirus or distemper, and I decided to give her a parasitical in case she had picked up some kind of infection while living on the streets. James held her while she was on the exam table, assuring her in a calm voice that everything would be all right. When we were finished, he lifted her off the table and asked her to give him her paw before pulling out a biscuit from his huge jacket pocket. He turned his bright smile on her, his even, white teeth contrasting with his dark-colored beard and mustache. He called her "my good girl," informing me that Suzy always had to work for her treats. Asking my permission first, he gave Cotton a dog treat as well. He reminded me of a misplaced missionary or a Peace Corps volunteer, and it dawned on me that my impression of the homeless had been based on stereotypes.

Suzy was a good and healthy patient, and I advised that they return in two weeks for a follow-up injection to ensure her immunity. When James asked for his bill, I told him not to worry about it until the next visit. He reluctantly agreed because I insisted. After they left, Ro and I shared our enthusiasm about our new clients, their fabulous coats, and how well spoken and polite James had been. We asked ourselves how anyone so seemingly responsible and intelligent could be homeless. I also asked myself how I could let my dog accept food from a complete stranger.

Two weeks later, James and Suzy were right on time and in the waiting room when Cotton and I got to work. There were several other clients waiting, and although they were seated at a respectable distance from James and Suzy and their shopping cart, everyone shared in a conversation about their pets.

Suzy stood bravely for her vaccination and after I encouraged James to have her spayed at some future date, he once again volunteered to pay his bill. I refused to accept his money, telling him to use it to feed himself and Suzy. Once again Ro and I remarked about what a gentleman James was and how odd it seemed that he lived on the street. If any of my other clients had been put off by James's presence, none of them mentioned their displeasure to me.

Several weeks later I received a phone call from a distraught client. She had noticed a homeless man with a dog tied to his shopping cart. From her description, I knew it wasn't James. At various times when she'd passed the man, he had been delusional, yelling and threatening passers-by as his dog cowered behind him. She was concerned about the dog's welfare and, together with a group of animal lovers, had kidnapped the dog. She had placed the dog in a temporary foster home, but wanted to know if I knew of anyone interested in permanent adoption.

The newspaper ran a human-interest story about the kidnapping titled, "Who Stole the Bag Man's Dog?" There was no mention that the victim might not be a suitable owner for his missing pet. The story was instead focused on finding and returning the dog. I knew this woman to be a rational, loving pet owner. I supported her decision and was happy to hear that the dog had been placed. Throughout this ordeal, I never asked myself if Suzy might be better off with someone else. From the moment I had met them, I felt that she and James were right for each other.

Fall went by quickly. Christmas was around the corner and Cotton wore sweaters to protect her still-naked chest from the chill. One day, James and Suzy came into the waiting room unannounced. I thought that something might be wrong with Suzy, but James told me that they were simply paying a social call to wish me a Merry Christmas, and he handed me an envelope. Thanking him as I opened the card, I was stunned to see a crisp one hundred dollar bill inside. A big smile crossed James's face. I told him that I couldn't possibly accept his gift.

"Listen doc," he said, "you don't know how many people give me ten- or twenty-dollar bills when they see me on the street with Suzy, especially at Christmastime. Take that money for the other dogs that need help. We're in good shape."

Feeling awkward, but probably no more awkward than he had felt when I forced my charity on him, I accepted his gift, earmarking it for the next stray that was brought in. Cotton and Suzy shared a biscuit, and Ro and I wished the colorful pair a Merry Christmas and a safe and warm winter.

It was spring when I saw James and Suzy again. Their coats were gone, and although Suzy looked the same, James had been through a transformation. The ragged jeans he had worn were replaced by khakis. A canvas belt replaced the rope he had used before. He wore a button-down shirt and a sleeveless sweater vest. His long hair was trimmed to a medium length and was parted on the side. His beard was cut short and his nails were trimmed and clean. He looked like an older college student. I tried hard not to gawk. He wanted Suzy examined before having her spayed. Suzy, for her part, was as fine as ever and had even gained a few pounds.

Unable to restrain my curiosity, I asked James what was new. He explained that he had met someone on the street as she walked her dog, a large mixed breed she'd rescued from an animal shelter. The woman gave Suzy a treat each time she passed them and was a real animal lover, often bringing Suzy the contents of a doggy bag saved from dinner the night before. At first, James told me, he had shared the meal with Suzy, but after a while he felt dishonest sharing food meant for her. James and his new friend would sometimes walk their dogs together along the East River. With her encouragement, he found a job at a thrift store called Return Engagement, the profits of which went to support an ever-growing gang of stray animals kept on the premises.

"I would have never met her if it weren't for Suzy."

James and Suzy were now living in a rented furnished room. He was able to bring her to work every day as well. We scheduled a date for her surgery for the following month.

When they returned for Suzy's hysterectomy, it was obvious that James's metamorphosis was ongoing. His beard was gone, he carried a new Eddie Bauer knapsack on his back, and the penny loafers I had seen on his cart were now on his feet. But the biggest news was yet to come. James was engaged to be married to the woman who had befriended him and Suzy on the street. After the surgery, they were moving to the Midwest. Suzy would have a home with a yard and James planned to work and go to night school to finish his degree in social work. I wished James all the best and asked him to give me a forwarding address so I could send him Suzy's records. James heartily thanked me for everything, shook my hand, and squeezed my shoulder.

Cotton and Suzy sniffed each other for the last time.

That night as Cotton rode in her basket on our way home, I wondered aloud if James would have gotten off the streets if it hadn't been for Suzy. Cotton perked up her ears, tilted her head, but didn't answer.

XI   D O N N E G A N : Third Time's a Charm

Everyone in the neighborhood must have thought that
Dan was twenty-five years old, and his longevity could have
been a testament to my skills as a vet. The truth be told, he
was the third in a series of West Highland Terriers belonging
to the nicest, most charming senior couple in my practice,
the Geltmans.

Oscar Geltman was tall and erect with a shock of gray-
brown straight hair, a sharp nose, and a square jaw. A dashing
looking man with a merry demeanor, he never came to
see me without Connie, his "wife for life," as he called her.
Connie looked as if she could have been Oscar's sister, in the
way that older couples often come to resemble one another.
Her toothy smile and bright blue eyes—a match for her
husband's—were framed by a mass of curly silver ringlets.
They had been married for eons, as they put it. I never knew
if they had children or grandchildren, but they treated Dan as
if he were their son, and brought him to see me several times
a year. They were an inseparable trio. I often saw Oscar and
Connie walking arm in arm in Central Park being led by Dan

or driving to the country in their old convertible, Dan's nose pointing into the wind.

Retired and out of the work force for a number of years, they had no need for a working wardrobe, and bought all of their clothes from thrift stores. Perhaps they never threw anything away, because they wore an astonishing array of styles and fabrics that chronicled the passage of time over the past few decades. I wondered if Oscar was aware of his innate fashion sense when he wore seventies-style trousers in the nineties. Connie made an equally strong statement when she single-handedly tried to resurrect platform shoes a decade before their most recent resurgence.

The two of them radiated happiness, cheer, and a general exuberance for life. Connie, who had worked for the New York City Police Department for thirty-one years, was active in the neighborhood crime-stoppers organization. Oscar had become a ballroom dancer, frequenting competitions in upstate New York and Connecticut.

Their appearance must have caused quite a stir in the building where they lived, a luxury high-rise on East Seventy-ninth Street with a concierge, a circular driveway with a fountain, and a clause in their lease that said that when Dan passed away, there could be no new dog.

And so when Dan's breathing became labored and he developed a cough from a leaking valve in his heart, we all began to worry. We knew that medication couldn't keep him going forever. The low-sodium diet and restricted exercise helped relieve some of the symptoms, but the day finally came when we had to let Dan go. The Geltmans were very brave. I assumed that as older people they had faced death and dying more often than most. When they told me they wanted Dan's ashes so they could bury him at their little house in the country, I made the arrangements.

Before they left, Connie asked me if she could drop by the office from time to time to sit and visit with Cotton. My heart went out to them. Did it occur to them as it occurred to me that one day soon one of them might have to help the other out of this world and face life alone?

Within a week and much to my surprise, the Geltmans were back for a visit with a new Westie, a male about four years old. They entered the exam room with matching smiles.

"Who's this?" I asked.

"Why, it's Dan the Second," explained Oscar, who was sporting a jaunty plaid scarf around his neck.

They explained that they had found him in a shelter in Connecticut after they buried Dan the First. They hoped that a mature dog, rather than a new pup, might fool the doorman and the neighbors into thinking that this was the original Dan. Of course, they would have to give the new Westie the same name if they were to pull off their ruse.

It worked! No one questioned the first Dan the First's disappearance, or his reappearance in a slightly smaller but friskier form. The Geltman family was complete once again.

Dan the Second was a healthy, active dog in spite of being initially diagnosed with heartworm, a mosquito-borne infection of a blood parasite that lives in the chambers of the heart. The treatment is rough and consists of a series of arsenic injections that kills the worm and takes a lot out of the dog as well. Dan the Second came through it and thrived, however, and no one suspected that he was an imposter.

There are advantages to being a white dog. Dan the Second grew older and whiter and looked the same. But as the Geltmans aged I could see changes in them. Over the course of their frequent visits, I watched as Connie walked with a cane while Oscar sweetly supported her. We always brought a chair into the exam room for Dan's checkups—no waiting in the car or in the waiting room for Connie. She wanted to be present and often repeated the same questions about Dan's health. I couldn't believe how quickly time passed. It seemed like Dan the Second had turned thirteen overnight. Oscar said he was drinking gallons of water and was unable to control his bladder. I drew blood and the tests confirmed that Dan the Second was in kidney failure. I gave Oscar the test results over the telephone. He didn't want Dan the Second to suffer, so he made the final appointment. I was amazed by how peaceful Oscar and Connie were, and that made me feel much more comfortable with our decision. I wondered if this sense of tranquility and wisdom came with age. If so, I looked forward to finding it.

As I thought about the two Dans, it occurred to me that perhaps there had been a Dan who had pre-dated the first one I had met over seventeen years before. The transition between Dan the First and Dan the Second had been easy. Once again, the ashes were boxed and buried underneath an old star magnolia tree in the country.

I worried about the severity of their loss. How could Oscar and Connie live without Dan? It would be impossible for them to get another dog because Oscar had to devote so much time to taking care of Connie. Oscar wasn't immune to the passing of time either. I knew he still went swimming every day at the health club in his building, and still drove his Buick convertible back and forth to Connecticut, but I wondered if this was wise.

Against all odds, Oscar and Connie surprised me once more. Dan the Third came from a shelter on Long Island, generously funded by a vacuum cleaner mogul with a soft spot for stray animals. I broke into a grin as wide as Oscar's when the three of them shuffled into my exam room. The visit was perfunctory as this was a bouncing pup of three years. "You had Dan the First and Dan the Second, why don't you call this one Danagain?" I suggested. "It has a Gaelic ring to it, and only the three of us will know what it really means."

And so Danagain became Donnegan, and life continued along on its steady cycle.

* * *

Oscar visited me recently in response to a card we had sent reminding him of Donnegan's boosters. The dog looked great and Oscar was fine except that his mismatched thrift store bargains were more dotted with food stains than usual.

"I'm going to be ninety-one this month," he told me.

"Wow, that's great," I said. "Happy birthday!"

"I swim every day," he said. "I think I'm getting faster."

"I know," I said. "You've told me. You're amazing. How's Connie?"

"She passed away last November."

I was speechless. Oscar continued, "It was very fast— a stroke. I splashed her face with cold water but her eyes wouldn't blink." The explanation seemed rote, as if he had repeated it numerous times before.

His eyes filled with tears. "It's really better . . . she was having such a hard time . . . really better this way. I just have to keep busy." He held Donnegan to his chest and continued, "I've started painting. I'm taking a class. I'm not half bad." That familiar smile crept back into his face.

"That's great," I stammered, stunned by this sad news. "Do you have any family in New York?"

"Yes, a sister," he said. "She's older than I am. And of course, there's Donnegan. He keeps me going." He absentmindedly stroked Donnegan's head.

I sent Oscar a birthday card later that week.

XII   S H E L T I E : Sole Companion

I passed a man on the street one morning—a man I had often passed before—who was walking his two sable shelties. He had made an impression on me, this small, short, balding man. He never hurried his dogs along and was tolerant of their constant sniffing and stopping. His diminutive size was in proper perspective to that of his two companions.

He always dressed in casual clothes, and I wondered if his dogs were a focal point of his retirement. He spent a lot of time talking to fellow dog owners on the street, introducing his well-behaved charges to others and enjoying the canine conviviality. Cotton and I never made their acquaintance but always acknowledged the man with a nod.

This particular morning, however, the man was only walking one dog, and I was stunned by an awareness that he had lost one. My first impulse was to ask where the other dog was, but we had never spoken before. To interrupt him now would seem to disrespectful. I stopped though, without saying a word, to watch them pass.

He was walking quickly, the eastern sunlight illuminating his face in what looked like a grimace. His features seemed contorted, rearranged, and his body seemed twisted as well, his neck held at a slight angle from his shoulders. His right leg, out of sync with the left, bowed outward with each step as he listed forward.

At the end of the leash, the solitary sheltie struggled to keep up with his owner's uneven shuffle, the collar straining at the base of his skull, pulling his graying snout forward.

I felt a familiar surge of sadness and fought back a tide of tears. Though they were held together by a four-foot strap of leather, they weren't really connected to one another. Each was isolated in a world of loneliness and pain, lacking the cohesiveness that I hoped they would one day rediscover.

XIII C O T T O N I I I: The Dog of My Life

Cotton died on June 16, 1990.

I had not yet lost a parent or a sibling, although friends around me were dead or dying from AIDS, and my father had been diagnosed with Alzheimer's disease. None of this added any perspective to my loss.

By the time she was thirteen, I had cleaned Cotton's teeth three times, and I took a certain measure of pride in the fact that she had not lost even one molar. As I was preparing her for her fourth dentistry, I noticed that she had a quiet heart murmur. She displayed no outward signs of discomfort, no cough or shortness of breath, and she could still run up to two miles with me. I listened again and again, not wanting to believe that I was hearing a small leak from a malfunctioning heart valve. I called in Dr. Lowe to listen, and she confirmed my diagnosis. A hot-cold wave of anxiety flushed through me. An inescapable feeling of panic knotted my stomach.

Cotton trembled on the exam table, sensing my nervousness as I stumbled along the path I now shared with those clients to whom I had to deliver bad news. What made this time different from all the other times was that I possessed the knowledge of where this bad news would lead. I knew what dilemmas Cotton and I would endure, and about how much time we had left together. Facing her mortality was overwhelming even though I'd faced similar situations a thousand times before in my work. I struggled to suppress my premature sense of grief, and vowed to do everything I could to keep Cotton healthy and comfortable.

Unrelated to her heart condition, Cotton began to have muscle tremors. The first few moments of her morning walks were marked by a vigorous tremor in her rear legs as she waited to cross the street or stopped to sniff a lamppost. She reminded me of a car that idled too quickly, needing a carburetor adjustment. It didn't seem to affect her in any other way. Cotton was still Cotton, chugging away, walking her ten blocks to the office or riding in her basket. But I saw the tremors as yet another reminder that as an older dog she was not going to be with me forever.

I have always told my clients that as dogs age they still run and play, but less often and for shorter periods of time. This was true of Cotton. When we played chase with her tennis ball, she returned it less often and with a little less enthusiasm or was content to just lope after it until it stopped. She often lost sight of the ball once it stopped moving, so I would run across the lawn and retrieve it for her, which seemed to please her. At the beach, she raced along the shoreline in a madcap run, the thinning fur on her erect tail blowing in the breeze. But the distances she ran grew shorter.

On Mondays, Cotton slept through much of the day. Clients asked if she was okay when she didn't extend them her usual warm greeting when they walked in the door. She usually picked herself up by the end of the week, demonstrating some of her former enthusiasm for her hostessing duties or resuming her self-assigned responsibility to concentrate on our resident parakeets.

Walking to and from work, Cotton became interested in sniffing her surroundings more than ever. I wondered if this was a delaying technique, if she needed more time to stop and rest. Perhaps she was becoming more interested in what she could perceive through her nose. Maybe her sense of smell was becoming stronger as her other senses faded. I had to call her several times to rouse her from sleep or vigorously shake my keys to get her to come out from under the bed when it was time to go outdoors.

On one of the rare occasions that she chose to sleep under the bed covers, I reached to pull her close to me and was shocked to feel how cadaverous her frame had become. I hadn't let myself realize until that moment that she was suffering from cardiac cachexia—that is, her muscles were atrophying from lack of oxygen due to her failing heart. I put her on a regimen of cardiac glycosides and a low-sodium diet that she dreaded. Soon she couldn't manage the walk to work, so I carried her each day in the bicycle basket.

On one of our shortened walks, I felt a tug on the leash behind me and turned, only to find her partly conscious on the street, her heart too weak to propel her forward. We made it home without further incident, but I knew I had to brace myself for what was sure to come.

Dogs, in my experience, do not have a sense of death. They simply exist in the moment. They don't seem to fret about the future or concern themselves with the past. The present is the strongest tense. When another animal dies in the hospital, there is no communal response from the others, no silence, no excitement, no heightened sense of perception, at least none that I have ever noticed. Cotton did not know that some day she would leave me and never return. But I knew.

Late one Friday morning, Cotton suddenly vomited under the counter behind my exam table. But this was not an ordinary vomiting episode. After retching for a few moments, she fell on her side and started to labor for breath.

I sprang into action, inserting an intravenous line into her skinny forearm and injecting a diuretic to clear her lungs. Struggling through a maddening sense of helplessness, I applied nitroglycerin ointment to her refashioned earflaps to lower her blood pressure and reduce the strain on her heart. Through it all, she continued to pant and struggle for air. She flopped on her side several times, taking deep breaths with a look of pure panic on her face. Perhaps she had torn a blood vessel or ruptured a ligament within her heart. My dog was dying before my eyes.

I knew what I had to do.

I held her head in both my hands and looked into her eyes. Kissing her snout, I told her that I loved her, sobbing as I delivered the concentrated barbiturate into the dog I had loved for eight wonderful years. She relaxed as her fading heart slowed and then stopped. I held her in my arms, her familiar weight and shape already changing. After a little while, I let my assistant take her from me. Then I went home to put away her bowls and coat and leashes. A little while later I returned to work, deciding that it would be the best way to get through the day.

That night I made sounds I never knew I could make, and I swore off dogs forever. For weeks I cried along with the owners of other dogs I put to sleep, reliving again and again the anguish and the anxiety of losing my own. Misery and grief surrounded me.

I realized that it was important for me not to forget Cotton. I made a scrapbook with her pictures and condolence cards that I could never find the courage to look at. I put her ashes in a small mahogany box, which I kept under a lamp in my living room. I said goodnight to her every night when I turned out the lights, but after a while I began to forget to do this. The day finally came when I felt my loss had lightened. It no longer shadowed everything I did and took up a smaller place in my heart.

It took me nine months to find Cotton's successor. My new dog's name is Billie, a bichon frisé. I am in love with her, although in a different way than I was with Cotton. I am profoundly surprised by how uniquely different Billy is, but am even more astonished at the way the human heart is able to gently blur memories, allowing us to go on repeating this cycle of love and loss again and again.

XIV K I K I : The Dog of My Future

Not so long ago, I flew to West Palm Beach to visit Mom for Thanksgiving. As I walked off the airplane I wondered if my Mom would be there to meet me. Mom had recently lost Klute, her beloved Shih Tzu. Before the visit, Jerry, Mom's husband of forty years, had warned me that she had been crying every day for six weeks. When I saw her, I knew that underneath her trembling smile she was in the depths of despair.

Although she protested, saying that she couldn't own another dog, we started telephoning local pet shops to locate Shih Tzus for sale. It turned out that Mom had been tracking the new arrivals of Shih Tzus at the Puppy Palace, a strip mall pet shop in Boyton Beach. It was there that she delightedly chose a seven-week-old puppy that she eventually named Kiki, for no other reason than it came to her—maybe because it was another name that started with a "k," like her beloved Klute.

She threw herself into taking care of her new charge with great enthusiasm, and after I returned to New York we talked several times a week about Kiki's progress, or lack of it. The new puppy's worst characteristic was that she couldn't tolerate being left alone, and would soil her crate or trash the kitchen if locked in there by herself.

Kiki's best trait was her tireless devotion to Mom. She followed Mom from room to room, lying at her feet as she worked the crosswords at the kitchen table, waiting on the bathmat as she showered, and sleeping at her side while she watched television. I visited several times a winter and was surprised to see how Kiki had followed in the footsteps of Klute with a maturity one wouldn't expect from a puppy.

Kiki kept Mom active and engaged. Every day, they went for one long walk around the condo complex, despite the fact that Mom had a back injury that left her with a limp. She met new neighbors who stopped to admire her puppy and talked to friends who were accustomed to seeing her with Klute. She spent at least half an hour each day grooming Kiki on a towel on top of the dryer in the laundry room, the puppy patiently allowing Mom to turn her and brush her thoroughly. She was a beautiful puppy with large brown eyes and remarkable lashes, and a dark, raccoon-like mask that eventually faded to white. Mom's hair was totally silver and she had always been complimented on her lovely brown eyes. I laughingly told her that she and Kiki resembled each other and that no one could tell that Kiki was "adopted."

In our family, there was an unspoken understanding that Kiki would probably outlive Mom. Twelve years earlier, my brother and I had promised to take care of Klute if that was ever necessary, but with Kiki the topic was never broached.

Mom was not without some guilt about accepting a new puppy into her life so soon after the loss of Klute.

She reminded me that Klute's death still felt fresh to her. I wondered if she thought about her mortality and perhaps had decided not to spend too much time grieving.

When Kiki was six months old, Mom and Jerry faced the extra expense of the puppy's hysterectomy. As it was, my Mom, a habitual smoker, was buying discounted cigarettes at the local reservation to save on taxes. The name-brand cigarettes she had formerly enjoyed were out of reach on her fixed income, as was anything else other than the basic necessities. After I made arrangements with the vet in Boynton Beach, I told a friend of mine that I was the only son I've ever known who had given his mother a hysterectomy for her birthday.

Jerry loved Kiki but, as was the case with all their other dogs through the years, he was not her primary caretaker. When he walked her, he would let her out the door on an extended leash so that she could reach a patch of grass while he stood inside. He would not take her for walks publicly and once said that he felt foolish walking a small dog down the street. I think he thought it made him appear feminine.

Every day, Jerry and Mom took Kiki for a ride to the farmer's market or to the grocery store for an outing, whether they really needed anything or not. Kiki rode on my Mom's shoulders between her neck and the headrest, their long hair commingling, both of them content to be in physical contact with each other.

On rare occasions when Kiki had to be left alone, Mom always had a talk with her. "Kiki, Mommy has something to tell you," she would say. "I have to go out for a while, but I'll be right back." Kiki would cock her head, listening, and then go off to her bed soothed by the explanation.

Mom prepared Kiki for my visits by telling her daily for a week, "Tommy is coming!" Kiki was always pretty excited by the time I'd get there, and each morning I'd wake to find her waiting at my bedroom door, anxious to jump into bed with me. She would flatten her whole body against my torso and push her face into mine with a strength that didn't seem possible for such a small dog.

I'd take her for longer walks than she was used to, encouraging her to run and go beyond the boundaries of the gated community she had walked with Mom. My impression was that this young pup was definitely under exercised. We played tug-of-war, tussled with each other on the floor, and she chased balls that I threw for her. I wanted to give her more diversions than she was accustomed to in her daily life. We formed a bond based on exercise and activity, a mutual physicality.

I rarely traveled to Florida in the summer, so Mom and I kept in touch by telephone and e-mail. Her short e-mail messages were always upbeat and light, although on the telephone she would sometimes comment about Jerry's crumbling mental condition or her own recurrent insomnia brought on by a lingering cough. I pleaded with her to see a doctor but she refused, saying she was switching doctors and would make an appointment when the paperwork was finished. I couldn't convince her over the phone and resolved to confront the situation on my next visit.

I decided to surprise Mom with an impromptu visit. When I deplaned, I was surprised that Jerry met me at the gate. He was slightly confused about which route to take home, although he had driven back and forth to the airport many times. When we arrived home, Mom greeted me with open arm and looked as glamorous as ever. She seemed to be smaller when I wrapped my arms around her, though. Kiki was overjoyed to see me.

Mom still managed to work her culinary magic and I could see that she was maintaining the dog, her home, and herself as well as ever. But that night, I found her panting and breathless at 2:00 AM on the couch in the den. She didn't go back to sleep until her breathing had returned to normal several hours later.

When I talked to her about making an appointment with a doctor, she told me that she had some X-rays two weeks earlier but hadn't yet received the results. After I returned to New York, I telephoned her doctor and was stunned by the news. Mom had an inoperable lung tumor. The doctor didn't know why she hadn't been informed, but said that he would call her himself since it would be inappropriate for me to deliver the news. He talked about the possibilities of chemotherapy and radiation, saying she would get more "bang for her buck" with radiation.

Later that day, Mom called me with fear and surprise in her voice to tell me what I already knew. Through tears, I telephoned my brothers, hoping against hope that we could come up with a solution and find someone or some procedure that could put off the inevitable. I worried that Jerry was not up to the task of seeing Mom through the physical, medical, and emotional challenges that faced them both.

Mom died on May 5, her birthday, while undergoing lung surgery. Although I had hoped for the best, I was relieved that she didn't have to suffer any longer. In one of our conversations in which I tried to convince her to go forward with some form of therapy, she said to me, "Tommy, I can't live forever." Those words soothe me still. I felt a consolation that she left us in total control of her faculties. She was able to do things that were important to her right until the end: cooking, keeping her house, maintaining Kiki, even driving her much loved red Miata convertible.

Jerry had difficulty handling the loss, and I wasn't sure he would be able to take care of himself. He often made phone calls to his kids, asking if they had seen my Mom. Within a few months, he and Kiki moved into an independent living facility in nearby Delray Beach. The space was much smaller than he was used to, but much more manageable.

For most of the first year, Jerry didn't interact with the neighbors or take his meals in the common dining room, and he didn't eat much of anything except potato chips. Kiki was his only companion. I called him often and encouraged him to meet people by walking Kiki. I sent him books on tape and tried everything I could think of to help, but he was unable to pull himself out of the rut he had slipped into.

When I went to visit him, I found Kiki and Jerry glued to each other. Kiki gave me an enthusiastic greeting but remained by Jerry's side for the most part. Scratch marks on the door, however, indicated that she had been frustrated and unhappy by being left alone. A basket of toys and one of Mom's slippers lay in the corner of the living room. Her hair was matted and dingy-looking. Clearly Jerry hadn't been brushing her. Not only that, but he never walked her either, and only let her outside on an extended leash while he waited inside. All weekend long, I made excuses to take her out for exercise and by the end of my stay Kiki and I had reestablished our bond.

Jerry's diminished short-term memory was apparent. He wasn't sure how long I had been there or how long I was going to stay. His side of our conversations was often parrot-like, and he repeated the same questions and answers within a short time frame. Most amazing was that the anniversary of Mom's death had passed without his mentioning it.

By midsummer it was impossible to reach Jerry by telephone. Whereas before he had always been at home, now he never seemed to be there. I called several times a week and left messages, hoping he was out walking Kiki or at least that he was out socializing with other seniors. But I in my heart I knew that wasn't the case. Whenever I did reach him I would ask if he'd been checking his messages. "Oh," he would reply, "do I have an answering machine?" Our infrequent conversations were superficial and short, and he invariably ended them by telling me how much he missed my Mom.

In New York, I imagined Kiki lying under the bed for hours. Between the dust ruffle and the wall, she would drift in and out of a fitful sleep interrupted by her own barking. I imagined that she was unable to find comfort squeezed between the pillows of the couch or behind the overstuffed chair. Perhaps she still smelled the now-fading scents that reminded her of Mom, the constant friend who she had loved, and who had loved her. I fantasized that when she awoke, she was aware only of her own ravenous hunger and wouldn't comprehend that eighteen hours had passed since Jerry's last visit. I conjured up images of her waiting by the door for hours and hours, expecting Mom to come home with Jerry. But instead Jerry would walk into the apartment with a woman who didn't seem to know that Kiki was even there. No matter how much Kiki wagged her tail or rolled over on her back before this woman's feet, she couldn't provoke a response of any kind.

It was time for a visit to see what was up in Florida.

I called Jerry when I landed in West Palm Beach and, of course, there was no answer. I was sure had had forgotten about my arrival. I parked near his sun porch, away from the main entrance to the building. The screen door was open, but the glass door was locked. I could see into the dark living room, and knocked several times, to no avail. Maybe he was out walking Kiki, I thought, somewhat relieved. Then a white fur ball streaked across the room and hurled itself against the glass. It was Kiki, jumping and scratching at the door, barking all the while.

I crouched down and told her I would be right back, then I ran to the reception desk. The concierge recognized me and told me that Jerry was most likely at Miriam's, that they were "an item" now, attending exercise classes together and even the opera—both firsts for Jerry at age eighty-three. As for the little dog, well, no one had seen much of her.

The concierge rang Miriam's apartment and I waited. I had not come to Florida to meet Jerry's new girlfriend. He had another thought coming if he planned on my taking both of them to lunch and dinner. I also considered the choice that Jerry had obviously made between an isolated, solitary life with Kiki and an active social life with Miriam, a human companion. I could not blame him, though I was filled with conflicting feelings about his loyalty to my Mom's memory. I was desperate to get back to Kiki, who clearly needed attention. Jerry and Miriam finally appeared, beaming as they shuffled their way to me.

Ever confident that no one could compete with my Mom's handsome beauty, I was stunned by Miriam's blonde radiance. Jerry's wide smile matched hers as he hugged me and then made awkward introductions. We headed toward Jerry's apartment on the other end of the building. At almost ninety, Miriam walked hesitantly as Jerry supported her arm in a gentlemanly way, and I suppressed my urge to run to Kiki. After what seemed like forever, we arrived. I could hear Kiki desperately scratching the door as Jerry fumbled with his keys.

Inside, Kiki raced madly around us, overjoyed to have company. As I dropped to the carpet to greet her, I was overwhelmed by the noxious smell of ammonia in the small space and I noticed yellow stains leading to the patio exit.

Kiki was much thinner and her hair was unkempt and completely matted to the skin. The situation was worse than I had thought.

We settled in the living room, Jerry flanked by Miriam on one side and Kiki on the other. Miriam, a widow who had recently given up driving, hailed from New York, where she had worked as an interior designer. She had children and grandchildren "up north," but had never had a pet and wasn't particularly fond of dogs, although she described Kiki as "darling." She spoke in the faded, husky voice of the elderly but had the perpetual smile of an ingénue.

Despite myself, I warmed up to her, and was able to put aside any feelings I had about her taking my Mom's place in Jerry's affections. I found myself agreeing to have lunch with them in a restaurant. Reluctantly, I left Kiki behind. On the drive, Jerry asked me where we were going at least three times. Having lost most of his hearing, he asked Miriam to repeat herself over and over. I wondered for a moment why he wasn't wearing hearing aids and then remembered that six months ago Kiki had eaten them, no doubt out of a desperation born of hunger or boredom, or both. Throughout lunch Jerry repeatedly pinched Miriam's cheek and caressed her chin, telling me how lucky he had been to have loved Mom and then to have found someone else he could love. They confided to me that they wanted to get married. I noticed that Jerry never referred to her as Miriam, but as Pretty Lady or Honey. Later, when we were alone, he admitted that no matter how hard he tried, he just could not remember her name.

With Jerry's permission, I took Kiki to the vet's office to be groomed. The staff greeted her warmly and sympathetically. They were aware of Mom's death, but were surprised by the condition of Kiki's coat, which had to be shaved to the skin. They offered to help find her another home if Jerry couldn't take care of her, and confided that this was not an uncommon scenario at their clinic.

On the ride home, Kiki surprised me by climbing up behind my shoulders and riding on my neck. She was waif-like without her fur, although the vet had said Kiki had only lost less than a pound. Her eyes, no longer hidden by fur, looked even larger than normal. She bestowed a look of pure love and admiration upon me, and I wondered how would I be able to leave her behind, alone and lonely and uncared for.

Later that afternoon, Jerry's son Lloyd came to visit with his wife, Carol. They hadn't been in the apartment for a while, as they were in the habit of picking up Jerry in the lobby. They were shocked by the stench in the air and the utter destruction of the carpet. Carol was particularly unsettled, as she had worked side by side with Jerry to furnish and set up the apartment. I mentioned to Lloyd that I had been unable to reach Jerry by telephone and they told me that had had been sleeping at Miriam's for the last two months. Kiki slept at home, alone.

Dinner was a repeat of lunch. Miriam was dressed, coiffed, and manicured. Jerry was ecstatic at her side, thrilled to have loved two beautiful women in his lifetime. Holding hands, they were like two sixteen-year-olds on a date, focused only on the moment and each other. I asked them point-blank what they intended to do with Kiki when they married, and Jerry told me he hadn't thought about it. It was clear that Kiki wasn't a priority for him.

Home by 8:30 PM, I escorted them to Miriam's apartment. Jerry said he would be home later, but I knew he would forget what he said. I called Lloyd and Carol to explain the situation more fully to them. Kiki could not be left alone all night indefinitely. Eventually her psyche would be damaged and her housetraining permanently lost. She wasn't receiving the care she needed. Eventually they gave me their permission to take Kiki back to New York with me. Now I had to confront Jerry.

Jerry returned to the apartment Sunday morning and was surprised to find me there. Kiki, in a display of loyalty, greeted him animatedly as he bent to greet her. Calling her "my Kiki-bird," he offered his lips to her heartfelt licks. This wasn't going to be easy.

"Jerry, we have to have a talk."

I explained my feelings to him and reminded him that if I had not been there, Kiki would have spent the night alone. She had spent too many nights alone already, I told him, and pointed to the stained rug, and the deep scratches on the living room door. Suggesting that my Mom would want the best for Kiki, I said that I wanted to take Kiki back home to New York with me.

"That would kill me," he responded tersely. "She saved my life."

"Do you think Miriam might change her mind about Kiki?" I asked. "About wanting to help take care of a dog?"

"Maybe," he answered. "Maybe someday. But she's not really a dog person."

"Jerry, we don't know when that someday might be," I said. "I think it would be best if I took Kiki back to New York."

Our conversation took a different turn and although he hadn't given me his permission, he hadn't said no either.

My time in Florida was running out. I was booked on the first flight out the next day. My choices were either to take Kiki home with me, which felt like kidnapping at this stage of our negotiations, or to leave her in an intolerable and inhumane situation.

That night, we had dinner at a French restaurant of Miriam's choosing. She had vichyssoise and Jerry had duck. They shared profiteroles for dessert. I said my good-byes to them in the lobby, explaining again that I was leaving early. Jerry made no pretense about coming home that night.

At the apartment, I wrote a long letter to Jerry reminding him of our earlier conversation. I packed a few of Kiki's toys and spent a sleepless night watching time crawl by, telling myself that I could change my mind at the last minute. Kiki slept peacefully at my side.

With guilty resolve I left Florida with Kiki the next morning.

Kiki and I have been together ever since. Within days of our New York arrival, she stopped reacting with alarm to every loud noise on the street. She and Billie, my bichon frisé, took to each other and eat and sleep side by side.

I worried that Billie would be jealous, having been the "only dog"—after Cotton—for fourteen years of my life. But perhaps she accepted Kiki because she had become accustomed to sharing me with so many patients at the office. I'm not sure that she differentiates between home life and office life and maybe for that reason Kiki doesn't seem like an interloper. After all these years as a veterinarian, I can't say I truly know what dogs think.

For a long time I was uncomfortable in my role as kidnapper/savior. Jerry was upset that I had taken Kiki home and called me several times only to hang up after he confirmed that she was with me. I consoled myself by considering the alternative. Eventually, we resumed our former friendly relationship. I continued to have difficulty reaching him on the telephone even though I would call him at Miriam's. They were married in the fall.

Having Kiki has changed my perspective on the loss of Mom. Being able to hold in my arms a living link to her memory has softened my grief. I am sure she would have approved of my decision to bring her dog home with me. As for Kiki, her connection to me runs true and deep. I wonder if she remembers Mom and their life together and has any sense of continuity now that she lives with me. Is there something that nurtures her canine soul and allays any fear of abandonment that may linger? I hope so.

Kiki will be the dog that I grow old with. Kiki is the dog of my future.

XV B I L L I E : A New Life

I'd come to Croton-on-Hudson—a small village forty-five minutes outside of New York—to see two litters of puppies, which were born about ten weeks ago. This litter was to be the first of many puppies that I would look at in search of Cotton's replacement. No pet shop puppy for me. Not only did I want a healthy dog, but I also longed for a perfect specimen as well, perhaps one good enough to be shown, although truth be told, I couldn't imagine myself in a show ring. With the perfect bichon frisé, I imagined making a name for myself as *the* bichon frisé veterinarian.

Cotton had been gone for nine months. I always knew I couldn't replace her, but as I'd heard many times before, once a pet person, always a pet person. I was going to do my homework, research the field, and take my time. After all, not only was this was to be the first dog in my life I'd ever paid for, but it would also be the dog I'd spend the next fourteen or fifteen years of my life with. I wasn't in a rush to decide anything on the spot.

As nine little curly white creatures scrambled around the chrome legs of an ancient dinette set, I felt my resolve dissolve. Most of the puppies were wrestling around, chasing each other's tails, and mouthing each other's muzzles. But one puppy had found her way to my shoes and engaged herself in a frantic game of tug-of-war with my shoelace. I lifted my leg, dragging her toward me. The shoelace was firmly clenched between her jaws, and her paws dragged against the flooring. "You're choosing me," I said. "I'm not choosing you. Right?"

Her black button eyes glistened, fixed on the task at hand. Her stare remained unbroken as she kept the tension on the shoelace. "Boo Boo," I said, my nickname for any unknown dog, "let go and come see me." I picked her up, held her from her front legs, and sized her up. She was a surprisingly solid dog. Holding her to my chest, she licked my chin. Her warm puppy breath made me smile.

"Right now she looks as if she could be show quality," said Nadine, the breeder. "The stud is from an Australian line. I'm not sure what his pups will turn out to be." Nadine housed only two bitches and claimed to breed them only once a year—a hobby that helped her pay for incidentals for her three kids.

"I could let that puppy go for eight hundred dollars," she said as she absentmindedly picked a bit of mucous from one of the bitch's eyes.

A wave of panic rushed over me. I was actually considering buying the first pup I cradled! I couldn't commit to fifteen years of responsibility right there on the spot, yet the thought of leaving her seemed impossible. "Can you hold her for forty-eight hours?" I asked.

On the way back to the city I waged a psychological game of tug-of-war with myself. I barraged myself with all kinds of questions: Was I ready to begin all over? I'd never raised a dog from puppyhood before. Should I adopt a dog that was already housebroken? Would I care that much that if she didn't turn out to be show quality?

I returned on Monday evening, a towel-lined carrier in the passenger seat, eight one hundred dollar bills folded neatly in my wallet. I considered turning back a few times, but it was time to take the plunge and have a dog of my own again.

As I drove back home, my nameless puppy licked my fingers as I curled them through the carrier gate. I already knew I had made the right choice and was caught off guard by feelings of protectiveness, pride of ownership, and kinship.

I named her Beany after the cartoon character from *Cecil and Beany*. My brother's name was Dean; we called him Deany as a little boy, so perhaps on some level I was naming my newest little charge after him. My friends universally hated the name (no wonder I had never met a dog called Beany before). Even my girlfriend Penny thought the name was less than charming. She counseled me to choose something similar in sound since Beany was already responding to her name. My friend Michael suggested Billie, which was somewhat similar to Beany in sound and had the added caché of being slightly androgynous. It was also the name of three great predecessors: the singer Billie Holiday, the actress Billie Burke (Glynda the Good Witch of the West from *The Wizard of Oz*), and the athlete Billie Jean King, depending on your pop-culture barometer. Bean became her middle name, making her officially Billie Bean DeVincentis.

* * *

I dedicated myself to paper training Billie. To ensure success, I set my alarm each morning to 3:00 AM and pulled Billie from her crate in the kitchen and put her squarely in the middle of the floor, which was entirely lined with newspaper. She was rewarded for her efforts with a small piece of Lorna Doone cookie—my preferred training treat—and soon we were down to only one two-foot by two-foot swath of newspaper.

As soon as the cold spring weather broke, I took her for rides in my bicycle basket. She seemed to take to it very quickly. However, I soon realized that unlike Cotton, who became mine at a more mature age, Billie would need more exercise since she was a growing pup. I decided to walk her to work rather than ride my bike as I had with Cotton. Billie learned how to sit and give her paw by the time she was four months old and although a mind is a terrible thing to waste, I never taught her another command in her entire life. Eventually, I could encourage her to bark at almost nothing by inciting her to "give 'em hell." One day, I brought Billie to Bridgehampton, Long Island, to show her off to my friend Bob Brooks. Bob was raking leaves near his newly opened swimming pool, which was full with black water from the previous year's debris. Billie, excited to be in such a wide, open space, ran in circles around the pool as we admired her puppy energy. When she cut a corner too sharp, she fell into the deep end of the pool and sank beneath the scummy surface and disappeared. Assuming she would surface, we let a few seconds go by, waiting for her to come up in an instinctive dog paddle. The seconds felt like an eternity, however, and Bob and I plunged in feet first to find her. I brought Billie home. She was cold, slimy, and shivering. I bathed her and waited to see if any of us would be diseased for life from our plunge beneath the foul pool water. Luckily, we were all fine.

With time, Billie developed into an avid athlete, although she never did take to swimming. To build her stamina, I took her on fast walks and short runs. This put a bit of a cramp in my own jogging style but eventually she was able to accompany me on three to four mile runs through the corn, wheat, and potato fields, which checkered the Hamptons. We would also run the circumference of the Central Park Reservoir or around the park's Sheep Meadow. Billie loved to run off leash, following a scent. If she ever lingered behind, she would sprint to catch up to me. I thought such exuberant displays would leave her exhausted but surprisingly, once we arrived home, she would pick up a tennis ball and drop it at my feet, ready for more action. Billie was proving to be an appropriate name since she was such a tomboy.

One morning, I took Billie running with Michael, who was always impressed by her stamina. We had finished a thirty-minute course that took us through a field marred by construction of soon-to-be large wood-shingled houses dubbed McMansions. These McMansions were cropping up all over the Hamptons, and just as their nickname would suggest, they looked exactly like one another. It was as though the

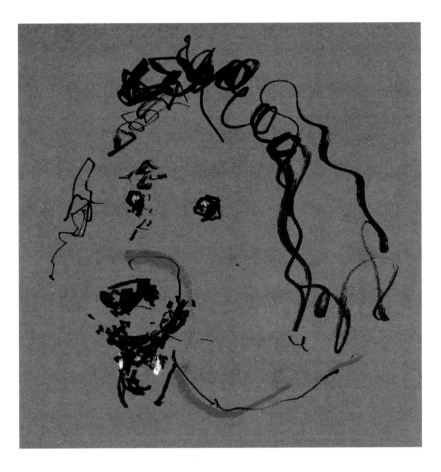

Hampton's housing development had been super-sized. As we approached our home, we lost sight of Billie, who had fallen behind. I wasn't worried about her disappearance. She often found her way back to the house before me. More than once, I'd see her tiny form sitting atop the front porch as she'd patiently wait my return down the long and narrow driveway. Suddenly, though, Michael and I heard a high-pitched squeal. Pivoting around toward the sound, I saw what appeared to be a white blur turning and twitching on a grassy mound in the distance. The white blur had to be Billie. It appeared as though she were fighting with an imaginary adversary. Her body flipped from side to side as she yipped, the sunlight fading behind her.

Michael and I ran to her aid, half expecting to find her in the jaws of a raccoon, possum, or even worse, a fox. To our shared amazement, Billie was lying on her side, whimpering and exhausted. The band of a steep leg trap bloodlessly gripped the hock of her left rear leg. I dropped to the ground, my hands trembling uncontrollably. I held her as Michael tried to pry the jaws apart. The movement only intensified her pain and for the first and only times in our shared lives, Billie bit my hand.

The strength of the trap amazed us and we both struggled to pry it apart. Expecting broken bones or lacerations, I was surprised and grateful that her skin was not torn and nothing was broken. I rushed her home, but Billie was inconsolable. She walked on three legs and immediately hid under the bed. She would not come out for dinner and refused to look me in the face as I tried to reassure her. The irrational thought occurred to me that she somehow associated me with her painful experience. Astoundingly, she appeared on all fours for breakfast the next morning. Feeling that she needed a treat for her ordeal, I added slices of chicken to her bowl. Later that day, I called the environmental protection agency as well as the police. When we went o remove the trap, it was no longer there. Someone had obviously known to remove it. The summer I sported a Fur Is Dead bumper sticker on my car and distributed anti-fur literature in my office.

Throughout the years, Billie slowly filled the void in my heart that was left by Cotton's death.

* * *

My life with Billie has been a continuation of what my life was like with Cotton. We walk to work each day, drive to the country on the weekends, and visit the beach. She has made many friends at the office, both human and canine and has earned the moniker Nurse Billie. On Halloween, she once donned a nurse's cap made from a Styrofoam cup. She is, overall, very healthy and I can boast that at sixteen she still has every tooth in her head.

Until she was twelve years old, she ran three to four miles with me every weekend. She chased tennis balls until she was fourteen years old; then, sadly, she could no longer track their movement on the lawn.

The passing of time is less noticeable when you live with an all-white dog. There is none of the telltale graying to remind me that the years have gone by, just the occasional milky reflection from Billie's aging eyes and a slight diminution in her former enthusiasm. When did Billie become an old dog? I miss the pup that raced around the pool, barking frantically. I remember the days when she would jump on my chest in the morning and give kisses on command. When I go running with her now, which doesn't happen very often, I am saddened by the sight of a faded tennis ball hiding in the hedges or in the overgrown border of the perennial garden.

As I write this, Billie is sitting on the deck, a cool breeze ruffling her hair. She is gazing at the pool. Though her eyesight has gotten poor, I know she can smell the scent of chlorine and water. Does she remember the so-called swimming lesson I gave her or the day she got stuck in the steel trap? In the distance beyond the pool is the yard and field that we have walked and explored at least a hundred time together. Now all she does is sniff the wind.

I joke that Billie is in assisted living and I'm her attendant. I take her to work in a bag and carry her up the three small stairs she used to climb to get into our apartment. I no longer send her to the groomer, preferring to clip and bathe her myself, no matter how unprofessional the outcome. I walk her in a harness rather than a collar to lend her body more support as she sometime teeters on her rear legs. I've asked my hospital staff to give me a wake-up call if I ever become oblivious to the reality of Billie's condition. I'm waiting for a sign, a turning point, to alert me to things that I've always advised to my clients.

How can I predict how deep a hole this loss will expose in my life after our sixteen-and-a-half years together? Like all the other pets in my life, Billie gives me a feeling of cohesiveness to my life. Together with Kiki and Billie, I have an enriched sense of family. They, like all the animals I've had the pleasure to work with, give my life significance and have helped make me the vet I am today. Without them as my guideposts, work would have no meaning. Thankfully, for me, it does.

Acknowledgments

A big thank you to veterinarians Chantal Acosta, Lewis Berman, Peter Kross, Judy Mulder, and my staff, including Rose, Mike, Leslie, Tommy, and Audra. I would especially like to thank Ro Ronchini. Special thanks, too, to Marta Hallett, Signe Bergstrom, and Colleen Daly, for their encouragement; Michael Clinton, for his support; and Allison De Vincentis, for always making me laugh. The publisher and author would like to extend a very grateful thank you to Katrina Charmatz, who thoughtfully contributed her father's memorable and beautiful illustrations.

Illustration credits